P. S. Med.

THE
COMMON MARKET

27 . 1 . 62

THE SIX
COMMON MARKET
COUNTRIES

Stuart R. de la Mahotière

THE
COMMON MARKET

A COMPREHENSIVE GUIDE

HODDER AND STOUGHTON

The EMMWOOD cartoons, "Interviews on joining the Common Market" on Pages 15, 17, 19 and 21, are reproduced by kind permission of the *DAILY MAIL*, London.

© 1961 by Stuart R. de la Mahotière

FIRST PUBLISHED NOVEMBER 1961
SECOND IMPRESSION DECEMBER 1961

MADE AND PRINTED IN GREAT BRITAIN FOR
HODDER AND STOUGHTON LIMITED, LONDON
BY C. TINLING AND CO. LIMITED, LIVERPOOL,
LONDON AND PRESCOT

FOREWORD

by

Lord Gladwyn, G.C.M.G., G.C.V.O., C.B., British
Ambassador to France, 1954-60. United Kingdom
representative at the United Nations, 1950-54.

I AM very happy to welcome the publication of this work
on the Common Market by someone who can obviously
see the problem so clearly both from the French as well
as the English point of view. It will also be apparent that
Mr. de la Mahotière is *un homme engagé* and that he has
no doubt at all that Great Britain must, in her own
interests, join the European Economic Community. His
spirited defence of his thesis will appeal to some if not
to everybody but, whichever side they are on in the
present "great debate", all will welcome this acute and
sensible analysis of the problem.

Nobody who reads Mr. de la Mahotière's work with
attention can accuse him of underestimating the difficulties which may have to be surmounted before the United
Kingdom can sign the Treaty of Rome. In particular,
the formidable problems which will face such countries
as New Zealand and Australia are not minimised in any
way. Some may even think that the possible long-term
advantages for Commonwealth countries in the event of
Great Britain joining the Common Market have been a
little obscured by the very proper emphasis laid on the
immediate disadvantages for certain sections of inter-
Commonwealth trade.

All these matters, however, form the subject of negotiations between the United Kingdom and the Six. There are very few people who believe that the Government could recommend the signature of the Treaty of Rome by this country without any conditions, and I have no doubt that Mr. de la Mahotière's book will help those perplexed citizens who may find it difficult to make up their minds in the coming months on whether their rulers are going too far or not far enough as regards concessions during their discussions with the present members of the European Economic Community.

GLADWYN

London, November, 1961

CONTENTS

INTRODUCTION ix

1. The Common Market—What it is.. .. 11

2. The Common Market—What it is doing .. 24

3. The Future of the Common Market .. 49

4. Britain and European Unity 62

5. Application for Membership 71

6. The Reasons for Joining 78
   New Zealand, Australia, Canada, India,
   Pakistan, Ceylon, Malaya, Ghana, Nigeria,
   Rhodesia, Eire, Industry, Agriculture

7. Sovereignty and the Treaty of Rome .. 119

8. What the Parties and the Unions Think .. 128
   Labour Party and the Trade Unions
   The Liberal Party
   The Conservative Party

9. What They Say 139

   APPENDIX I—Vital Statistics 146

   APPENDIX II—Principal Clauses of the Treaty
   of Rome 148

"With access to the EEC we have the possibility of solving our problem, and maintaining the high standard of living in this island. Without it the prospect before Britain is of being pushed increasingly into a backwater. We shall, no doubt, from our backwater, continue to claim the respect that is due to the leader of the Commonwealth. But if we cannot earn our keep, it will be an empty title. What good did it do the Sultan of Turkey, in the end, to be the Caliph of Islam?"—LORD PLOWDEN and SIR GEOFFREY CROWTHER (in a letter to *The Times* on July 18, 1961).

INTRODUCTION

WAR destroys. But it also helps to bring forth new forms of political organisation, new institutions, new alignments. To go no farther back than the nineteenth century, the defeat of Napoleon brought forth the "Concert of Europe", the defeat of France in 1870 gave slow birth to the "Entente Cordiale". In the twentieth century, the "Little Entente", the League of Nations and the Rome-Berlin axis arose from the First World War. The 1939-45 war brought forth a multiplicity of organisations—the United Nations, the North Atlantic Alliance, the OEEC, Western European Union, the Coal and Steel Pool, etc. But none was more historically significant than the Common Market or to give it its proper name, the European Economic Community.

The Common Market is a unique and noble attempt by dedicated men to build a new Europe, not as Charlemagne or Napoleon had done, by force of arms, but by free negotiation between sovereign nations which had been all but destroyed in the holocaust of the Second World War.

Battling for years against prejudice and ignorance, against deep-rooted suspicions and animosities, traditions as old as the nations themselves, these men finally succeeded in laying the foundations of the New Europe —first with the Treaty of Paris in 1951, which set up the Coal and Steel Community, then with the Treaty of Rome in 1957, which gave legal shape to the Common Market.

The aim of both treaties is to unite Western Europe, both economically and politically. The political aims are long-term and implied. The economic aims are immediate and precise. The Treaty of Rome has already been in operation close on four years. Much progress towards unity has been achieved.

Britain cannot ignore the reality of the New Europe. The plant is taking root. Its growth, precarious at times, is there for all to see. What should Britain's attitude be? Should she join or stay out? This is the great issue of our times, as great for us as the Free Trade question or the Irish problem was for our forefathers. Whatever the decision, it will be historic. It cannot be shirked. If we stay out, we perpetuate the economic and ultimate political division of Europe. If we join, we abandon some of our most cherished institutions. Centuries-old traditions may be sunk overnight in the Channel. The Government are well aware that history must soon be made and it is ultimately the people of Britain who must make it. The modest aim of this book is to help them to do so.

Chapter One

THE COMMON MARKET—WHAT IT IS

THE Common Market is essentially the brain-child of that brilliant French economist, M. Jean Monnet. But it would not have been born without the skill in political midwifery of such good Europeans as Dr. Adenauer of Germany, M. Robert Schuman of France and M. Paul-Henri Spaak of Belgium.

After the war M. Monnet was charged with the herculean task of restoring France's industry and economic life which had either been shattered by five years of war or distorted by the German occupation. He succeeded magnificently and today France's economy, while not a model of efficiency, is unquestionably sounder than it has been for decades.

But even while France's economy was convalescing, M. Monnet was thinking how to build the new Europe. Years of experience had convinced him that if Europe was to recover something of its former greatness it could only do so by uniting both politically and economically.

Political unification seemed out of the question in the days immediately following victory, when passions ran high and bitter memories ruled the thoughts of men. But economic unification seemed not only plausible but indispensable. How else could Europe hope to compete with those two economic giants—Soviet Russia and the United States of America? So he worked out a plan for the unification of Europe by stages. First, there would be a modest beginning by pooling Western Europe's iron, coal and steel resources, then, step by step, the whole of Europe's economic resources—and indeed working manpower—would be pooled in a Common Market. Lastly, but some way off, a United States of Europe would emerge. In this Economic Community the emphasis would be on efficiency through rationalisation, through the removal of all artificial barriers to trade, through the elimination of restrictive practices, monopolies and cartels. In short, the "New Europe"—the "Brave New World" of the new generation—would have a planned economy which must inevitably lead to a planned overall policy.

M. Monnet started this uphill battle with the fervour of a dedicated "European", a man convinced that his was the only way to salvation. He gathered around him a group of like-minded men from France, Germany, Italy, the Netherlands and Belgium, all of whom had in some way come under his spell or had been inspired by his ideals.

In 1950 Britain was asked to join in bringing forth the first of the new communities, the European Coal and Steel Community. When Britain (under a Labour Government incidentally) refused, for reasons which will be fully explained in a later chapter, the group decided to go ahead on its own.

The 50-year Treaty instituting the High Authority of the Coal and Steel Community, known as the "Schuman Plan" at the time after M. Robert Schuman, the French Foreign Minister, who sponsored it, took just under a year to negotiate. It was signed in Paris in April, 1951 by the same countries which are now members of the Common Market, France, Western Germany, Italy, Holland, Belgium and Luxembourg and started to operate in July, 1952. M. Schuman called it "a bold and constructive first step" towards European unity. It meant that the production and distribution of all Western Europe's iron, coal and steel were in the hands of a virtually independent High Authority. Without these raw materials, no nation in Europe could make war independently. Yet by obtaining them as cheaply and as conveniently as possible, each nation's economy could move forward as rapidly and efficiently as possible.

The next step in building the new edifice of Europe, the Common Market, was held up for some time for political reasons.

In the 1950s the Americans decided that Germany had to be re-armed for the defence of Europe. This decision, a major one in American foreign policy, met with strong opposition not only in France and the Low Countries but in Britain as well.

When it was clear that the Americans would not be deflected from their course of bringing Germany into the defence plans of the North Atlantic Alliance (NATO), the French worked out a scheme whereby Germany would be re-armed not as an independent nation which might easily be ushered into NATO through the back door (she was actually admitted in 1955 through the front door) but as a member of what was to be called the "European Defence Community". How laboriously the EDC plans were worked out and finally adopted only to be thrown out by the French National Assembly is a long and painful story. Suffice it to say that the failure of the French Parliament to ratify the EDC dealt a severe blow to M. Monnet's plans for a United Europe. It showed that political unity, which meant also unity in defence, was a long way off. All the more reason, he thought, why the plans for economic unity should be speeded up. Otherwise the "New Europe" might be still-born like the EDC.

The long-term political implications of economic unity were not as obvious as those of the proposed EDC, whereas the material benefits it would bring in the shape of greater prosperity and a higher standard of living would be obvious to all.

The planners therefore decided that the time was ripe for the Powers (France, West Germany, Italy, Holland, Belgium and Luxembourg) which had joined the European Coal and Steel Community to consider what further steps towards unity could be taken, bearing in mind that the EDC, which would have been a short cut to political unity, had collapsed under the passionate onslaught of political opinion and sectional interests in France.

The "Six" met at Messina in Sicily in June, 1955, to discuss firm proposals for a far-reaching advance towards European economic integration, and an atomic energy pool. The Common Market was taking shape. The Messina conference charged a small committee, led by M. Paul-Henri Spaak, to work out the details of a new treaty to set up the "European Economic Community", the second milestone on the road to unity (the ECSC being the first).

Two further meetings of the Six Powers were required before the Treaty could be drawn up in its final form. The first was held at Venice in May, 1956, the second at Brussels in July of the same year.

Finally, an historic occasion, the Six Powers met in the Italian capital on March 25th, 1957, and signed the Treaty of Rome which gives legal shape and force to the Common Market and its subsidiary, "Euratom", the European Atomic Energy Community.

The first thing to remember about the Common Market is that it is 170 million strong. It is the largest single trading area in the world, larger even than the United States or Soviet Russia. Its rate of expansion is greater than that of any other West European country. Industrial production rose by 7 per cent in 1959, by 12 per cent in 1960. In 1961 a 7 per cent increase is expected. Overall production in the Common Market will reach American levels by 1975. During the decade between 1950 and 1960 industrial output in the area now covered by the Common Market increased by over 90 per cent. During the same period production in America increased by 39 per cent and in Britain by only 29 per cent.

Brig.-Gen. GULLY SQUARE-LEGG, M.C.C.

(President Empire Umpires' Club)

"They'll be wanting us to play French cricket next, dammit!"

The Common Market is the world's largest importer. It imports more even than the United States.

It produces more steel, more motor-cars and more manufactured goods than Soviet Russia. The forecast is that by 1975 the gross national product of the Common Market countries will have doubled compared with 1960.

All this is being achieved because, over and above the long-term political ideals which they have set themselves, the Common Market countries have two essentially practical aims. The first is to do away with all customs duties and other barriers to trade as between themselves as a bloc, the second to establish a common external tariff (as low as possible) between themselves and the outside world.

The original intention was that all barriers should be removed within twelve to fifteen years of the signing of the Treaty of Rome in 1957. But such has been the success of the policies pursued that the aim now is to have the Common Market programme completed and the Community fully operative by 1965 or 1966.

The full objectives of the Common Market are best illustrated by summarising the preamble to the Rome Treaty:

> The Six signatory nations intend to establish the foundations of an enduring and closer union between European peoples by gradually removing the economic effects of their political frontiers. A Common Market and a common external tariff (Customs Union) will be established for all goods; common policies will be devised for agriculture, for transport, for labour mobility, and for important sectors of the economy. Common institutions will be set up for economic development . . . all these measures will have one essential aim: the steady improvement in the conditions of life and work of the peoples of the member-countries.

The Common Market really is a "Community" within itself. It has:—

GLORIA SLUGGIT

(Miss Hornchurch 1961)

*"I think it'll be a super market—all them French
credit squeezes and that!"*

1. An ASSEMBLY composed of 142 members drawn from the Parliaments of the Six countries.
2. A COUNCIL OF MINISTERS consisting of one member from each Government.
3. A EUROPEAN COMMISSION—the executive organ of the Community—composed of nine independent members appointed by the governments of the Six.
4. A COURT OF JUSTICE composed of seven judges.
5. An ECONOMIC AND SOCIAL COMMITTEE which is a special consultative body.
6. A EUROPEAN INVESTMENT BANK.
7. An OVERSEAS DEVELOPMENT FUND.
8. A EUROPEAN SOCIAL FUND.

The composition of the ASSEMBLY is weighted according to the size and importance of member-countries. France, Italy and Federal Germany have 36 members each, Belgium and Holland 14 each and Luxembourg 6. Its functions are to exercise a general control over the work of the Community, based on the annual report submitted by the Commission.

The COUNCIL OF MINISTERS is the body responsible for co-ordinating the economic policies of the Community and for ensuring that decisions are carried out in each country individually. It acts mainly on proposals submitted to it by the European Commission. It can either reject or approve these proposals by a majority vote. It cannot amend the Commission's proposals except by the unanimous vote of those actually voting. Abstentions in this case do not count.

When the Council votes on proposals submitted to it by the Commission it resorts to a system of weighted votes which gives 4 votes each to Germany, France and Italy, 2 votes each to Belgium and the Netherlands and 1 to Luxembourg. Any 12 votes are required to carry a resolution binding on the Council. When the Council is voting on a proposal or resolution *not* submitted by the European Commission, it reaches decisions either by a

FRED UPPE

(Secretary Fish Porters' Union)

*"I don't want ter be a member of no * ! ! * ! ! * Common Market, mate!"*

simple vote, i.e. 4 votes out of 6, or by a weighted vote which must include a favourable vote by at least four members, the weighting being the same as that which applies to proposals submitted by the Commission.

The type of voting required is laid down in the Treaty according to the importance attached to a particular subject. For instance, decisions connected with (a) The transition from Stage 1 to Stage 2 in the implementation of the Treaty, (b) Agriculture, (c) Transport, (d) Extension of the legal powers of the Community, (e) Agreements with Third Parties, (f) Admission of new members require a unanimous vote. Generally speaking the Council will vote unanimously on vital subjects in the early stages. Thereafter most of its decisions, except those mentioned above and some others, will be taken either by a simple majority or by a qualified majority. This has the effect of strengthening the powers of the Commission.

THE EUROPEAN COMMISSION, the main executive organ of the Community, has wide powers in the day-to-day running of the Community. Like the Council, the Commission issues (1) Decisions binding on the parties concerned, (2) Regulations, the application of which is compulsory in all member states, (3) Directives which are also binding but which allow States a certain freedom of action in their application, (4) Recommendations and opinions which are not binding. All its decisions are taken by a simple majority. Its nine members, led by the Chairman, the German Professor Walter Hallstein, run the Common Market as a collegiate body. They are appointed jointly by the Six Governments and are chosen for their professional qualities and managerial capacities. They are usually economists or lawyers. They are expected to be, and are, completely independent. They neither expect nor solicit advice from their governments. They have their Headquarters in Brussels. No country can have more than two of its nationals on the Commission. They are of course subject to the overall supervision of

Rt. Hon. Mr. MACSKELL, M.P.

(Right Wing Socialist Independent for Dunderhead East)

"On the one hand I'm all for it. On the other hand, I'm not!"

the Assembly and the authority of the Council of Ministers.

THE COURT OF JUSTICE is composed of seven judges nominated by agreement. It serves the Common Market, Euratom and the Coal and Steel Community. When requested to do so, it gives rulings on violations of the Treaty of Rome or abuse of discretionary powers. It has already had two cases brought before it by the European Commission. Both were concerned with alleged infringements of Article 31 of the Treaty. In the first case Italy was accused of unlawfully suspending imports of certain pigmeats, in the second of applying the wrong import tariff on tubes and radio-electric valves for radio receivers.

The Court's rulings are binding on member Governments.

THE ECONOMIC AND SOCIAL COMMITTEE is another body which is common to the Common Market and Euratom (but not to the Coal and Steel Pool). Its rôle is consultative. Its members represent all sections of economic and social life within the Community such as employers' organisations, trade unions etc. They are appointed for four years by unanimous decision of the Council of Ministers. Their advice must be sought by the Council of Ministers and the Commission on certain matters as laid down in the Treaty. The Committee's composition is weighted: France, Germany and Italy have 24 members each, Belgium and Holland 12 each and Luxembourg 5.

The EUROPEAN INVESTMENT BANK. It has a capital of the equivalent of 1,000 million American dollars supplied in proportion to their financial capacity by all Six members.

It finances projects designed to assist the less developed areas of the Community. It also promotes modernisation and rationalisation schemes which would be beyond the means of individual members.

The OVERSEAS DEVELOPMENT FUND finances schemes for

improved education, public health and transport and industrial development in the overseas territories of member-countries. It can call on funds amounting to the equivalent of 581 million dollars during the first five years of its existence. Main contributors are France and the Federal German Republic, each giving the equivalent of 200 million dollars. It is of special interest to Africa.

The EUROPEAN SOCIAL FUND finances projects designed to facilitate the employment and mobility of labour within the Community. It irons out any dislocations and hardships caused to employers and employees by the reorganisation of industry under the overall plan for economic efficiency of the Community as a whole.

Chapter Two

THE COMMON MARKET—WHAT IT IS DOING

The European Economic Community was born officially on January 1, 1958, after all the member countries had ratified the Treaty of Rome.

It spent the first year of its existence setting up house —in Brussels—and getting its massive machinery into position and working. By the end of 1958 it had drawn up the most ambitious programme for economic expansion ever seen in Europe.

This programme called for:

(a) Common policies to encourage economic growth.

(b) A Customs Union brought about by removing all duties, import quotas and other barriers to trade between the Six as a bloc.

(c) A Common external tariff as between the Six and the outside world.

(d) Rules against price-fixing, restrictive practices, cartels, monopolies and other unfair trading practices.

(e) The introduction of a uniform 40-hour week.

(f) Equal pay for women.

(g) A minimum three-week holiday a year for all with pay.

(h) The retraining and rehabilitation of workers temporarily redundant or displaced by the freeing of trade.

(i) Common policies on wages and social insurance, unemployment benefits, etc.

(j) The free movement of labour and capital.

(k) The free movement of services such as banking and insurance.

(l) A completely integrated system of transport—sea, air, rail, road and inland waterways.

(m) Common policies for agriculture.

The purpose was simple: To make European industry more efficient and therefore competitive, with high wages for the workers and low prices to the consumer.

The first problem to be tackled by the Community was the reduction and progressive elimination of tariffs by the Six between themselves.

THE INTERNAL MARKET

The removal of tariffs and quantity restrictions by the Six between themselves was to take place in three stages of 4 years each, starting in 1958. In fact, this period is likely to be considerably shortened owing to the success of the Community's policies and to favourable economic conditions in Europe generally during 1959 and 1960.

During the first 4 years, tariff reductions were to reach 30 per cent of the tariff actually applied by each member on January 1, 1957; during the second 4 years they were to reach 60 per cent; they were to be abolished completely by the end of the last 4-year period. Export taxes, export subsidies and revenue duties on imports must all disappear by the end of the first stage.

In actual fact, the speeding up of the time-table after only three years and not the four years specified has meant that by the end of 1960 the cuts amounted to 30 per cent. And by the end of 1961 they are expected to amount to between 40 per cent and 50 per cent instead of 30 per cent. In other words, the process of reducing tariffs will be some two to three years ahead of schedule by the end of 1961.

The removal of quotas on imports was speeded up still further, and by the end of 1961 all quantity restrictions on imports applied by members between themselves will have been abolished.

Only agriculture lagged behind because it raised special problems in all countries. About 20 per cent of the EEC's population is engaged in agriculture. Some countries are large exporters like France, Holland and Italy, others are concerned to protect their home producers. And although, in principle, the rules of the Common Market will apply to agricultural products and foodstuffs, the Treaty in fact provides for a cushioning effect in the shape of controls, levies and minimum prices to be applied in the early stages in the case of many important commodities.

The system of agricultural protection is complicated but broad agreement has been reached on a common policy aimed at price stability and the raising of farming standards by greater mechanisation.

As a first step, farm products have been divided into three categories for the purposes of the common market and each category is being treated separately.

(1) *Wheat and other cereals, dairy produce and sugar.* For these, European Marketing Bureaux have been or are being set up and considerable control of prices and distribution is envisaged with protection through variable levies against external competition where necessary. Annual target prices are to be fixed and the Bureaux will become buyers if market prices fall below target prices.

(2) *Beef, pork, poultry and eggs.* Protective tariffs, minimum import prices, price support and variable levies will apply. A Bureau will co-ordinate the policies of the various national marketing boards, but there will be no target prices.

(3) *Fruit, vegetables and wine*. An external tariff applies, with import restrictions where necessary. Common rules of competition will apply with the uniform classification of certain grades and qualities of wine. There will be no Bureau.

Further items for which a tariff is being worked out are rice, oils and fats, fish and tobacco.

Consultative committees of experts are to be set up to advise the Commission on each item and on the working of the agricultural Common Market as a whole. Also, a "European Agricultural Guarantee Fund" will be set up to co-ordinate the work of the various Stabilisation Funds. In the case of cereals, dairy products and sugar, these items will be dealt with by Management Committees composed of the Managers of the various national organisations.

It is hoped that the Common Market in agricultural products generally will be fully operative by 1967 and earlier in the case of beef. Meanwhile a transition period is envisaged during which prices for agricultural products in the Six will be brought into line as far as possible. First steps in this direction were taken in 1960 and some painful adjustments were necessary. The price of wheat in France and Holland, for instance, rose, whereas it went down in Italy, Germany and Luxembourg. The price of maize rose in Italy but fell in France. Barley was cheaper in Germany but dearer in France.

Apart from the former French colonies in Africa which are now independent, and for which special provision has been made, most overseas territories of the Six enjoy the benefits of reduced tariffs on their exports—mostly agricultural products—within the Community without being full members of EEC. They are not subject to all the terms of the Treaty but are theoretically required to eliminate gradually the differences between the tariffs they apply to imports from the European country of which they are dependants and those they apply to imports from other members of the Community. They are allowed to retain certain protective and revenue duties.

The establishment of a common tariff between the Six and the outside world and the progressive lowering of that tariff is, on the economic plane, the final objective of the Treaty of Rome. It puts the roof on the Common Market edifice and takes the European Economic Community into an international field where every tariff move has a direct effect on the trading interests of those outside the bloc—even more so than the internal market because it enables the Community, with its vast industrial resources, to trade as a bloc and compete on world markets with countries like the USA, Britain, Soviet Russia, etc., individually.

The common external tariff is to be introduced progressively at the end of each of the three transitional stages provided for in the Treaty. Its application can be speeded up by general consent and, in fact, the first steps towards applying it were taken a whole year earlier than planned.

On January 1, 1961, the first alignment was made of each country's individual tariff on the common external tariff. This meant that in the case of low or medium tariff countries like Holland, Belgium and West Germany, some customs duties had to go up whereas France and Italy had to reduce theirs.

With certain exceptions, the Common External tariff is the arithmetic mean of the tariffs of each individual country as they stood on January 1, 1957, i.e. a year before the Treaty came into force. It will not exceed 3 per cent for most raw materials; 10 per cent for most semi-manufactured goods; 15 per cent for certain inorganic chemical products, and 25 per cent for a range of organic chemical products, dyestuffs and man-made fibres.

The exceptions are those for which the tariff is being

or has been negotiated with the other members of the GATT. They amount to about 70 items and affect about one-sixth of the imports into the Common Market by non-members. They include timber, petroleum products, fats, wood-pulp and machine-tools.

Bearing in mind that the Common Market aim is progressively to reduce all its tariffs with the outside world, the following duties of interest to the Commonwealth will apply at least in the early stages, unless altered by negotiation on the admission of new members.

TEMPERATE ZONE PRODUCTS—(of interest to Australia, New Zealand and Canada)—*Wheat*: variable levy probably equivalent to a tariff of 20 per cent; *Barley*: 13 per cent; *Meat*: 20 per cent (plus possible import levy); *Butter*: 24 per cent; *Cheese*: 23 per cent; *Aluminium*: 10 per cent; *Lead* and *Zinc bars*: 10 per cent (less on virgin metal); *Wood, Wood-pulp* and *Newsprint*: 5–8 per cent; *Paper* other than newsprint: 14–21 per cent; *Wool, Copper* and *Nickel*: Duty free.

TROPICAL AND SUB-TROPICAL PRODUCTS—(of interest to India, Pakistan, Ceylon, Malaya, Hong Kong and African members)—*Tin, Flax, Rubber, Oil-seeds, Hemp, Sisal, Jute*: all duty free. *Cocoa*: 9 per cent; *Coffee*: 16 per cent; *Tea*: 18 per cent; *Oranges*: 15–20 per cent; *Bananas*: 20 per cent. Cotton grey cloth and cheap textiles from India, Pakistan and Hong Kong are unlikely to escape duty of some sort.

During the early stages after the coming into force of the Treaty at the beginning of 1958, the Community naturally made it its first task to get the internal market and external tariffs under way. But work was also begun on all the other aspects of economic union—common trade policies and capital investment plans, the free movement of labour, capital and services such as insurance and banking, common policies on wages, collective bargaining, the resettlement of displaced workers, etc.

In doing all this the European Commission—in a sense

a superbody of nine wise men—had to avoid giving the impression that it was practising a disguised form of socialism whereas in fact its high-level planning was aimed essentially at producing a well-balanced economy through free enterprise and fair competition.

In working towards economic union in Europe and giving aid to the overseas territories and former colonies of its members, the Commission uses THREE main instruments: I. the European Investment Bank; II. the Overseas Development Fund, and III. the European Social Fund. It also works through various committees and sub-committees including the Advance Planning Committee, the Monetary Committee, the Control Committee, the Consultative Committee on Transport and the Economic and Social Committee. The latter, as mentioned above, has a special status of its own under the Treaty. So has the Monetary Committee which, in years to come, has a very important rôle to play in directing the economic affairs of Western Europe.

I. THE EUROPEAN INVESTMENT BANK.

Its statutes are modelled on those of the World Bank. It is run by a Board of Governors appointed by the Six Governments, a Board of Directors appointed by the Governors and an Executive or Steering Committee appointed by the Board of Governors on the recommendation of the Board of Directors. In 1960–61 its Chairman was Paride Formentini of Italy and its Vice-Chairmen were Hans Karl von Mangoldt-Reibolt of Germany and Claude Tixier of France.

The Bank's initial capital of $1,000 million was made up of the following contributions: France and West Germany $300 million each; Italy $240 million; Belgium $86·5 million; the Netherlands $71·5 million and Luxembourg $2 million.

The Treaty gives it power to raise funds on the international money market and to seek special loans where necessary from member states. It has already availed itself of this faculty, on two occasions. In March, 1961, it raised a private loan of 20 million Dutch florins in Amsterdam and again in June, 1961, it floated a loan of 50 million florins repayable in 25 years at $4\frac{1}{2}$ per cent. A syndicate of Dutch banks led by the Amsterdamsche Bank offered this last loan for public subscription in July, 1961.

The Bank's creditors are fully protected. The Bank's lending powers are limited to two and a half times its share capital. It cannot purchase holdings. It must carry reserves. It cannot incur exchange risks. The money it lends is protected by a guarantee from the government of the country to which loans are made or by some other form of security.

Since early 1959, when it started operating, the Bank has financed modernisation and improvement schemes to the tune of $100 million, representing a 15–18 per cent contribution to the total cost. These projects include:

1. Modernising the railway line between Chambéry and Genoa.
2. Rebuilding the stations at Modane and St. Jean-de-Maurienne.
3. Converting the electrified part between Modane and Genoa to direct current. (It had operated on alternating current since before 1914).
4. Power-stations, chemical plant and a clothing factory in Southern Italy and Sicily.
5. Hydro-electric power-stations in Sardinia.
6. An Iron and Steel works near Taranto to which the ECSC is also contributing. Output capacity: 2 million tons of steel a year.
7. A Diesel-engine factory being built by the Alfa-Romeo firm near Naples in conjunction with another firm from an EEC country.
8. Irrigation works in the South of France (in the Departments of the Hérault, Gard and Aude).
9. A power-station in West Berlin.

10. A dam and power-station for use by Luxembourg and German interests.

When all these schemes are completed they will provide further employment for 6,500 men.

II. THE OVERSEAS DEVELOPMENT FUND.

By far the major portion of the Fund's $581,250,000 capital is being used for technical and economic aid to Africa. All France's former colonies in Africa, except Guinea, have maintained their links with the EEC since they achieved independence. They had every reason to do so because until the end of 1962, when the Convention regulating their original relations with EEC expires, they will be able to enjoy all the benefits of close economic association with the EEC without incurring any of the political commitments. What is more, even when their links with EEC are given a more permanent shape, there is every reason to believe that they will continue to receive technical and material aid from the West, through EEC, without in any way committing themselves to the political aims of EEC.

The economic benefits they reap from the present temporary form of association are considerable. They are receiving an increasing flow of cheaply-priced goods; they will have large new markets for their own products; they can set up customs barriers and—provided they do not discriminate as between the Six—impose levies on EEC goods in order to protect their own existing or nascent industries. They are receiving large sums for investment from the Overseas Development Fund.

The strengthening of Europe's ties with Africa is one of the major aims of the European Economic Community (and of General de Gaulle, incidentally).

Parliamentarians from the 16 African states now associated with the Community (mostly former French colonies), met in Strasbourg in June, 1961, and laid down the general principles which should govern relations between all the newly-independent African states, including many of those now in the British Commonwealth. They are:

1. No political strings to technical and economic aid from Europe.
2. There should be a joint European-African parliamentary body.
3. African states should be directly represented at the seat of the European institutions.
4. Guaranteed prices and markets for their goods.
5. Technical assistance should aim primarily at training African technicians and experts.
6. Financial aid should be in the shape not only of grants but of long-term loans.
7. Stabilisation funds should be created to guarantee prices for certain raw materials exported to Europe (mainly bananas, cocoa, coffee, ginned cotton, ground-nuts, ground-nut oil, palm oil, palm kernels, sisal, phosphates, copper, manganese and chrome ores and concentrates).

The African and European governments concerned have found little to quarrel with in these aims and much has already been done to meet the above requirements. They fully recognise that Africa has special needs and that the full trade liberalisation measures of the Common Market could not apply to the African States without causing a considerable upheaval and in some cases considerable hardship and damage to developing industries.

Present Community policy is based on price support and planned markets. Tariffs have been reduced on African goods and, indeed, in France's case, her former colonies who trade heavily with her, enjoy preferential treatment. This, however, may not last long because Holland and West Germany are against preferences for African goods which discriminate against goods from elsewhere and particularly Latin America. Brazilian coffee is a case in point.

On the other hand, the Six are now encouraging the consumption of tropical African products in Europe. The Germans have been asked, for instance, to reduce their tax on bananas which brings them nearly $200 million a year. In Italy the heavy tax on unroasted coffee places an unnecessary restriction on consumption.

Commercial relations between the Six and Africa are expected to be on a sound basis, despite many painful adjustments, by the time the new forms of association are adopted at the end of 1962.

Meanwhile, by the spring of 1961, the Overseas Development Fund had made grants-in-aid to African states totalling $129 million, divided up as follows:

1. Education, professional training and welfare $16,620,000
2. Health services 18,819,000
3. Water purification and irrigation schemes 3,609,000
4. Town planning 7,122,000
5. Welfare and social research . . 11,457,000
6. Roads, ports and railways . 49,487,000
7. Agriculture, stock-breeding and fisheries 21,388,000
8. Industrial and agricultural research . 504,000

Quite naturally, the bulk of this aid went to the former French colonies or Trust territories, since they form the bulk of the African states now associated with the EEC.

Indeed, the Fund's capital of $581,250,000, which is to be invested over a five-year period dating from 1958, is to be allocated to the overseas territories, or former overseas territories, of member states in the following proportions: France $511,250,000; Netherlands $35,000,000; Belgium $30,000,000; Italy $5,000,000.

The Fund has been made up of the following contributions: France and Germany $200,000,000 each; Belgium and the Netherlands $70,000,000 each; Italy $40,000,000 and Luxembourg $1,250,000.

34

As part of the technical assistance, scholarships and grants have been awarded to selected African students to train in the Universities and Technical Colleges of the Six in Europe. Coupled with British and American training schemes this ensures that virtually all African technicians of the future are likely to be western-trained.

III. THE EUROPEAN SOCIAL FUND.

The Council of Ministers approved the rules of procedure of the Fund in May, 1960. The Fund started operations with a capital of $30,000,000 for the years 1960–61. It has drawn up plans to achieve all the social objectives set out in the Treaty of Rome. These include the co-ordination of the social policies of each individual member with particular reference to employment, labour legislation, conditions of work, vocational training, social security, the prevention of industrial accidents and occupational diseases, industrial welfare, trade-union rights, collective bargaining, etc.

The Fund has worked closely with the Economic and Social Committee on which the trade and professional associations of employers and workers are represented. It contributes 50 per cent of the expenses incurred by governments or employers' organisations in resettling or retraining workers temporarily displaced or put out of work by rationalisation schemes. It also contributes financially to the mobility of labour.

One of the first schemes it put into effect was the redeployment of nearly 10,000 Italian workers transferred from Italy to Germany and Holland. The bulk of these migrant workers went to Germany where they took up jobs in the building and catering trades, and in industry. The Fund sees that they are properly lodged and that they suffer no financial hardship from being transferred and that they benefit from the German and Dutch social security schemes. Mobility of labour plays a most important part in the economy of the Six. Since the war Germany has recruited a foreign labour force of nearly 500,000 men and has absorbed large drafts of Italy's surplus labour. By the end of 1961 she expects to have something like 1 million foreign workers on her farms and in her factories, by far the larger portion being Italian. The fact that the Italian is a hard worker has not escaped German employers, as indeed it did not escape the National Coal Board and British Trade Unionists in 1948 when Italian labour was imported into the mines of Britain.

Reports have been drawn up and submitted to the Council of Ministers on common wage structures, working conditions in industry and agriculture, labour costs, equal pay for men and women, the utilisation of manpower, etc. The Fund has sponsored housing projects for displaced or migrant workers.

. . .

Apart from these three main instruments, the Commission also works through various committees and sub-committees including the Advance Planning Committee, the Monetary Committee, the Control Committee, the Consultative Committee on Transport and the Economic and Social Committee. The latter, as mentioned above, has a special status of its own under the Treaty.

The Advance Planning Committee is concerned with forecasting economic and political trends and makes long-term plans for the economic future of the Community. It works in close co-operation with the Monetary Committee and the European Investment Bank, and, indeed, with the High Authority of the European Coal and Steel Community. Up till now it has had to deal with boom conditions within the Community—a fact which has simplified its task.

The Monetary Committee has come out with some forthright criticism of the tendency of some Western Powers not to co-operate in vital monetary matters on an inter-national level and member countries of the Community have not escaped its wrath. It was particularly critical of the decision by Germany and Holland to revalue the Deutschmark and Guilder respectively without con-sulting the European Commission. It has called for much closer co-operation and on a wider front between Com-munity members. The present imbalance in international payments, it says, could be avoided if member-nations (Germany presumably, among others) were less national-istic and more Community-minded. It says liberal trade policies by the Six as a bloc would help to restore equili-brium to international payments.

Even so the Committee has paid generous tribute to the vigorous economic growth of the Community. It has given much thought to the long-term economic problems of the Six, such as a common European currency, a common reserve fund and the free movement of capital. The Treaty also calls upon it to consider problems arising from turnover taxes, excise duties and other forms of indirect taxation. Industrialists and manufacturers of the Six are insistent that if they are to face free competition from their EEC partners they should all be roughly subject to the same level of taxation.

The Transport Committee has made only a modest start in helping to frame common policies for European transport. This is due to the complexity of the problem and to the fact that the Treaty is vague on how the Common Market aims are to be achieved in the realm of transport.

The general aims of the Treaty are that transport, like everything else, must be run on a community basis. This means complete integration, which in turn means that there must be complete freedom in the movement of goods and passengers across the various (rapidly diminishing) frontiers. Community carriers must be allowed to operate freely without any distinction as to nationality in any

EEC country. There must be no discrimination in the shape of preferential freight charges, hidden subsidies by secret agreement between carriers and government agencies, or unfair advantages to exporters by means of secret agreements between shippers and carriers (as exist in Holland, for example). Governments or state bodies must not abuse the monopoly they enjoy.

Indeed, the European Commission has interpreted this to mean that state transport organisations must eventually streamline their activities so that they become more competitive and able, ultimately, to operate on a commercial basis. These are long-term aims which are bound to raise political difficulties arising from deeply entrenched positions.

It will take some time for the Commission, the Transport Committee and the European Investment Bank to get down to the problem of planning the future needs of an integrated transport system. Co-ordination of road transport will raise serious problems because of the vast number of private carriers involved. Meanwhile, the Commission has issued regulations under the Treaty prohibiting certain freight charges which discriminated against the owner and/or shipper because of the national origin of his goods or because of the country to which his goods were being shipped. Unnecessary frontier charges are to be abolished or progressively reduced.

The Commission has made a start on implementing the provisions of the Treaty, which prohibit state-owned transport systems giving indirect support to certain sectors of the economy—agriculture is one—by means of preferential rates and conditions of carriage. The Treaty does, however, allow this practice to continue (not indefinitely) where the State takes a hand in aiding and supporting under-developed areas "or areas seriously affected by political circumstances".

Future regulations issued by the Commission will be based on the following assumptions: (a) that there shall be complete equality of treatment in all the six countries, (b) that all transport enterprises shall be financially independent and enjoy complete freedom of action (within the accepted limits laid down by the Commission), (c) that investment policies shall be co-ordinated and (d) that users shall have freedom of choice.

In planning the future transport network of Europe, the Commission can look back on the very substantial achievements of the various organisations set up in Europe after the war. It will, in a sense, carry on where they left off.

First the European Central Inland Transport Organisation set up immediately after the 1939-45 war, then the Inland Transport Committee of the Economic Committee for Europe of the United Nations, the Inland Transport Committee of the Organisation for European Economic Co-operation (OEEC), and lastly, the European Conference of Ministers of Transport, all took a hand in modernising and expanding Europe's shattered transport system. Today, when the Common Market takes over, plans have been laid for the electrification of all the main lines of EEC Europe, and most of the lines linking North-West Europe with South-East Europe via Marseilles or Genoa and through Switzerland to Vienna and Austria have already been electrified. By 1968 electrified lines will link Vienna with Venice and Trieste.

Diesel traction has also increased enormously. In some cases the "Trans-Europe Express", of fast Diesel trains linking many commercial centres and capitals in Europe is faster than air transport. At the end of 1950 only 166 Diesel locomotives were in use. By 1960 the figure had jumped to 3,500 of over 350 hp.

Work on Europe's motorways has also proceeded apace. It is calculated that by 1970 all the main industrial centres and capitals of the Six will be linked by fast motorways on which conditions of travel will be roughly the same everywhere.

The EEC countries have been more alive to the value

of inland waterways than has the British Transport Commission. During the next few years they propose to revolutionise inland transport in Western Europe by widening existing rivers and building new canals in Holland, Belgium, France and West Germany. When the work is completed 1,000-ton barges will carry bulk cargoes between Bremen, Hamburg, Basle, Vienna and Marseilles and the coal and iron-ore of Lorraine will go by water on the Moselle Canal to the Ruhr.

Under the "Mississippi system", French and Dutch barges push up to 9,000 tons up the rivers Seine and Rhine instead of pulling something in the region of 1,400 tons. When the Canal network of the Low Countries is widened the "Mississippi" system will be introduced there too.

Shipping and air transport are also due to come under the umbrella of the Common Market but because they raise special problems owing to the international character of the services they render, they will not be tackled until fairly late in the Commission's time-table for implementing the Treaty.

On the air side, five major European companies have stolen a march on the Common Market by forming "Air Union". They are Alitalia of Italy, Lufthansa of Germany, Sabena of Belgium and Air France and T.A.I. both of France. This "Union" goes far beyond the pooling agreements which have long been a feature of international air transport. It entails the pooling of output and the sharing of profits according to agreed quotas, the joint purchase of aircraft, joint overhaul and maintenance arrangements, and, most important of all, joint negotiation of international traffic rights and fare adjustments.

It is a formidable organisation and when the Commission gets down to the detailed examination of monopolies and cartels in respect of air services, it will have to decide whether any of "Air Union's" activities come within the scope of the prohibitions in this respect contained in the Treaty.

. . .

No picture of the New Europe would be complete without some reference to the achievements of those two other organisations which are closely linked with the Common Market: the European Coal and Steel Community (ECSC) and Euratom, particularly as Britain would be expected to join them if she joined the EEC, as they form part of the trio known as the "European Communities".

The ECSC was set up by the Treaty of Paris. It began its operations in August, 1952. It paved the way for the Common Market and Euratom. Its executive body is the High Authority composed of nine members appointed by the Six Governments. It shares the EEC's Assembly, Council of Ministers and Court of Justice. Its aim has been to achieve a common market in coal, iron, steel and scrap metal and this it has done very successfully despite many technical difficulties, political crises and opposition from vested interests. It allowed itself a five-year transition period during which, to avoid dislocation, some tariffs, subsidies and price controls were allowed to continue. This transition period ended in February, 1958, and the final stage in setting up the Common Market was reached with the introduction of the external tariff. This tariff was fixed at between 2 to 13 per cent *ad valorem* for the six members of the Community.

By 1961 the following results had been achieved:
1. All barriers to trade in coal and steel abolished.
2. Aids and subsidies eliminated.
3. The rules of fair competition and non-discrimination applied.
4. Transport rates radically altered so that international and internal rate schedules could be aligned.
5. Important changes introduced in the methods of coal and steel distribution.

ECSC statistics show that between 1952 and 1961 deliveries of ECSC steel to Common Market countries rose from 2,100,000 tons a year to 10,000,000 tons a year. Production records are constantly being broken, and exports by EEC countries to the outside world rose by 173 per cent between 1954 and 1960. In 1960 they amounted to 11,146,000 tons.

Community steel output in 1960 rose faster than world output. World output was 12·1 per cent higher in 1960 than in 1959. Community output rose by 15·3 per cent. Total production of steel in the Common Market countries in 1960 was 72,800,000 tons compared with 63,200,000 tons in 1959. World output of steel in 1960 was 342,000,000 tons compared with 305,000,000 in 1959. Thus in 1960 the EEC countries produced 21·3 per cent of the world total. In 1952, before the effects of the Steel Pool were felt, the percentage was only 19·7.

The largest exporters are France and Belgium (between 20–25 per cent of their total production). Their prices were not competitive five years ago but they are today. Britain exports on an average only 15 per cent of production.

A common external tariff has been introduced and the following have been abolished: Customs duties, quantity restrictions, currency restrictions, discriminations in transport rates based on the nationality of the consumer and the dual-pricing system whereby export prices differed from those charged to home consumers.

The High Authority has seen that rules of fair competition apply, but it has come up against some stiff opposition from steel and coal interests in breaking up cartels and monopolies and in reorganising Belgium's coal industry.

In many cases it has prevented cartels and concentrations from forming, particularly in Germany and France, either on its own initiative or when applications for mergers or tie-ups have been submitted to it according to the terms of the Treaty. In cases where the mergers or concentrations would have had a restrictive effect, they have been opposed. Where they tended to improve efficiency, they have been approved. Good examples of both cases were provided when the mighty German steel concern August Thyssen-Hutte AG sought to acquire a majority control over Phoenix Rheinrohr AG. This merger would have created the largest steel production plant in Europe. After spending a year preparing its case for submission to the High Authority, August Thyssen withdrew the application, probably suspecting that it was going to be turned down in any case. Mergers were however agreed in the following cases:

1. Dortmund-Horder Hutteunion, which produces about 2,540,000 metric tons of heavy steel plate, and Huttenwerke Siegerland, which produces 250,000 tons of sheet steel a year.

2. Alfred Krupp and Bochumer Verein, which brought the total crude steel capacity of Krupp up to 3,300,000 tons a year.

No sooner had the Community settled down than it drifted straight into the coal crisis which had been brewing in Europe since the end of the war. So long as there was slack to be taken up in fuel consumption, not enough coal could be produced. But as oil began to replace coal as a primary source of power so the sales of coal began to slacken off despite the continuous increase in the demand for power. Pits began to work short-time. Some were only partially worked. Others closed down completely. In one year (1957 to 1958) pithead stocks jumped from 2,600,000 tons to 22,700,000 tons.

France and Germany began to reorganise their coal industries just in time. But Belgium was caught right in the middle of the storm.

Early measures by the High Authority to solve the crisis in Belgium proved inadequate and subsequent emergency plans were vetoed by the Council of Ministers of the Community. Eventually the High Authority got its plans adopted. They called for a complete reorganisation of Belgium's coal industry. By 1963 production capacity (30 million tons in 1957) was to be cut back by 9,500,000 tons. This was done by streamlining some collieries where uneconomic pits or seams were discontinued, and by shutting down others. Between 100,000 and 150,000 miners made redundant were either absorbed by other pits or retrained for other jobs. The High Authority used its supranational powers to impose drastic remedies. It achieved concrete and lasting results.

Planning the future of Europe's coal production is now closely linked with the planning of Europe's power needs generally, a task assumed by the European Economic Community in close association with ECSC.

The High Authority has encouraged and partially financed investments in iron and steel reaching over $1,000 million. Its investment funds total $360 million. Its operations are financed by a direct levy of 0.35 per cent on an annual global output of coal, iron and steel valued at some $8,000 million. It has a Guaranty Fund of $100 million. It can raise loans on the open market.

Like the EEC, the Coal and Steel Community takes a paternal interest in its workers. It has brought coal and steel workers higher real incomes, improved housing conditions, greater freedom of movement within the community and made special provisions against unemployment. It has financed the building of 60,000 new homes. It issued its first "European Labour Card" in 1957, and an agreement between the Six was signed in 1957 providing for social security for migrant workers.

It has partially financed the retraining of more than 90,000 workers formerly in the coal industry, contributing a sum of $43 million.

It has allocated $8 million for research into industrial health, the prevention of accidents, etc., with particular emphasis on the effects of silicosis and pneumoconiosis.

The ECSC Headquarters are in Luxembourg. Ten nations have appointed delegations to it: Austria, Denmark, Greece, Japan, Norway, Portugal, Sweden, Switzerland, Great Britain and the USA. The British Delegation was set up in 1952. A standing Council of Association, set up in 1954, provides a permanent channel for consultation and, where opportune, for co-ordination of policies. An agreement on iron and steel tariffs signed in November, 1957, between Britain and the High Authority reduced tariffs by 10 per cent *ad valorem*, with alternative specific rates.

. . .

The agreement setting up a European Atomic Energy Community, known as Euratom, was signed at the same time as the Treaty setting up the Common Market.

Its aims are to finance and develop nuclear power for industry in Europe; to help meet the constantly increasing demand for electricity, to promote research and training of atomic scientists and technologists, to draw up common investment plans and, where necessary, to set up atomic installations of its own in the common interest.

Since January 1, 1959, Euratom has maintained a common market in nuclear materials and ensures equality of access to them. It ensures the free movement of labour and capital within the Community in connection with atomic energy projects and research. It has concluded agreements for research with private firms and also with nuclear establishments outside the Community.

It plans to spend $215 million from 1958–63 and double that figure in the following five years. It co-ordinates and promotes research by financing the building of new installations and the provision of equipment and supplies.

Its activities are concentrated on the supply of atomic energy for peaceful uses and particularly on the supply of electricity during the next decade when consumption in

EEC countries is expected to double. In 1958 the Six consumed 225,100,000 megawatt-hours—roughly the same as the Soviet Union. By 1980 nuclear generating capacity is expected to contribute 40,000 megawatts.

Euratom has taken steps to protect the health of atomic workers and to ensure that atomic stocks are not diverted for other uses. All stocks of fissile material held in the countries of the Six must be declared, and Euratom has its own inspection teams which can operate anywhere in the Community. It is the exclusive owner of all plutonium and uranium 233 stocks intended for peaceful uses and makes them available to private firms and member states.

Euratom's main research effort is centred on reducing the cost of nuclear fuel. Three distinct types of reactor development are being undertaken:

1. Graphite-moderated, gas-cooled systems already in use in Britain and France and the pressurised boiling water systems developed by the USA and the organic moderated type. New techniques are being developed to improve performance.

2. Types not yet proved but with good prospects of being used for power production. Work is proceeding on the building of a prototype industrial reactor of the heavy water moderated organic, liquid-cooled variety.

3. In conjunction with the Organisation for Economic Co-operation and Development (successor organisation of the OEEC) the high temperature gas-cooled Dragon project at Winfrith Heath, Dorset, England, and another advanced gas-cooled reactor being developed in France. The aim is to improve performance at higher temperatures.

It has established an Information Bureau on the use of Radio-isotopes in industry and medicine and is prepared to help in research and development in this field where necessary.

The following nuclear installations in Europe come under its wing:

Research Centres:

Grenoble
Saclay
Fontenay-aux-Roses
Cadarache (under construction)
Saluggia (Piedmont)
Ispra (Lake Maggiore)
Milan

Jülich (nr. Aix-la-Chapelle)
Wageningen (under construction)

Frascati
München-Garching
Karlsruhe
Frankfurt am Main
West Berlin
Casaccia (under construction)
Geesthacht (nr. Hamburg)
Arnhem

Mol (Belgium)
Petten (under construction).

Power reactors:

Trino (under construction)
Chinon (under construction)
Monts d'Arrée (under construction)
Jülich (prototypes under construction)
Mol (prototypes under construction)
Marcoule on the Rhône
Choos on the Maas in Belgium.

Kahl on the Main (prototype)
Garigliano
Latina

Mining Centres:

Ellweiler (under construction)
Vendée-l'Ecarpière
Grury-Gueugnon
La Crouzille-Bessines
Saint-Priest La Prugne.

Refining Centres:

Milan
Pierrelatte (France) (under construction) (manufactures uranium 235)

Malvesi (near Narbonne)
La Rochelle
Le Bouchet (south of Paris)
Olen (outside Antwerp)
Wolfgang (near Frankfurt-am-Main).

Fuel Element Manufacture:

Mol (Belgium) (under construction)
Olen
Herstal, near Liege
Wolfgang
Bonneuil-sur-Marne
Corbeville
Le Bouchet
Saint-Loubes, near Bordeaux (under construction)
Annecy
Milan

Irradiated Fuel Reprocessing:

Cap de La Hague (Cherbourg) (under construction)
Marcoule.

Euratom co-operates with the European Organisation for Nuclear Research (CERN) set up in 1954 by 13 European nations (Austria, Belgium, Denmark, France, West Germany, Greece, Italy, the Netherlands, Norway, Sweden, Switzerland, Great Britain and Yugoslavia). CERN provides for collaboration in fundamental nuclear research. Its laboratories are at Meyrin, near Geneva.

Euratom has entered into agreements with Britain, Canada and the USA. In 1958 the USA agreed to help finance the establishment in Europe of six to eight American-type reactors with a total capacity of 1,000 megawatts at a capital cost of $350 million, of which $135 million are long-term credits from the US Export-Import Bank.

In 1959 it concluded an agreement with the United Kingdom Atomic Energy Authority for the exchange of information and assistance in the design and construction of nuclear reactors and for the supply of fuel for reactors.

Chapter Three

THE FUTURE OF THE COMMON MARKET

THE Coal and Steel Community has been going for close on 10 years, the Economic Community and Euratom for 4 years. The ECSC has another 40 years to run. The EEC was set up for an unlimited period. All three Communities are therefore on the threshold of their tasks.

The first years have shown the most encouraging results. With a working population of some 73 million (out of a total of 170 million), production in all fields has risen sharply—spectacularly in the case of steel. Gross National Product (the total value of goods and services produced plus income from abroad) has gone up steadily. In 1960 it rose by approximately 6·5 per cent compared with 1959. Industrial production for the same period rose by 12 per cent, inter-Community trade went up by 25 per cent and imports by the Six from non-Community countries rose by 20 per cent.

The Community is second in car production only to the USA and produces proportionately more steel than Britain—73 million tons in 1960, compared with Britain's 24,300,000 tons. Large-scale investments will bring steel capacity in 1963 up to 82 million tons per year—an all-time record for Europe.

The removal of internal tariffs and the application of the external tariff are ahead of schedule. Integration has proceeded apace in some sectors. Commercial tie-ups and rationalisation in foodstuffs, the automobile industry, electrical household equipment, capital and consumer goods have brought cheaper goods to more people.

Although wages are generally higher in Britain than they are in the Common Market countries, real wages are often higher on the Continent owing to indirect benefits such as cost-of-living bonuses, larger family allowance, and more extensive national health benefits particularly in the long-term treatment of illness.

However, much remains to be done. The Commission's first concern was to implement the Customs Union and the common external tariff and this it has done ahead of schedule. But it has only just begun to tackle the thornier problems of integration, such as anti-cartel legislation, state-subsidies, common taxation, social and labour policies. It remains to be seen, for instance, whether in 1962 France's partners will follow her example and introduce equal pay for men and women for equal work and a uniform 40-hour week.

Common trade policies for the Six as a bloc and application of the rules of fair competition both at home and abroad raise the most complicated issues. A beginning, however, has been made on the subject of a common trade policy with the outside world. The Commission has succeeded in getting the Six Governments to agree to insert a clause in all future agreements and treaties with third parties stating that nothing in the document shall clash with their obligations under the Treaty of Rome.

The Governments will also supply regular information to the Commission about impending negotiations for the conclusion of new commercial agreements or treaties and will consult the Commission before signing. With certain exceptions these agreements will not extend beyond the transitional period of the Common Market, i.e., after 1970 or thereabouts. All existing trade agreements are being reviewed by the Commission to see whether they hamper in any way the formulation of a common trade policy.

Oil, tobacco and agriculture still force the Commission to tread warily in the pursuit of its aims.

A common market in oil can only be considered in

terms of a common market for energy generally. In other words the Commission must co-ordinate supply and demand for oil, coal, natural gas and atomic power. American and British capital is heavily invested in European oil. France is anxious to market much of the Sahara's oil and natural gas, both of which are being produced in increasingly large quantities (approx. 17 million tons of oil in 1961 and between 20,000 and 30,000 million cubic metres of gas forecast for the coming years).

Sahara oil is of the light variety—not of the heavy type needed for industry—which means that to be marketed successfully it must compete with the lighter oils sold by the British and American firms. Even so there is no reason to doubt that Sahara oil will be fitted into the general pattern of Europe's oil supplies, because consumption of oil never goes down. Proof of this can be seen in the vast network of pipelines and refineries being built all over the Continent. However, the activities of the resourceful Mr. Enrico Mattei, who has a finger in many oil pies in Europe, the Middle East and Africa must be an added complication. Mr. Mattei, who is head of the Italian State Oil Agency, "Eni-Agip", prefers to play a lone hand in international oil and has induced the Italian Government to refuse to limit imports of cheap Soviet oil. Moreover he is reported to have contacted the Algerian nationalists with a view to developing Sahara oil in the event of the partition of Algeria. He also has plans for the development of oil in Morocco and Tunisia which have not escaped notice in Paris and Brussels.

Again, the Commission has only begun to nibble at the state monopolies which, in the case of tobacco, matches and certain alcohols, bring in much-needed revenue to the exchequers of the Six. As a start, however, Community tobaccos, which are now facing increased competition from Greece, are being imported on a more competitive basis with state brands and can be bought more easily although not necessarily more cheaply.

As for agriculture, this was always considered one of the acid tests of economic integration. Although the Commission's modified proposals were in the end accepted in principle by the Council of Ministers, little or nothing was done for months to put them into effect.

Each Government has been interpreting the Treaty of Rome in its own way in order not to incur the wrath of its farmers. Britain is not alone in having an awkward, vigorous and vociferous farm lobby. The Germans have theirs, and the revolt of the Breton peasants in the summer of 1961 was a reminder to the French Government that French farmers were still not finding the outlets within the Community that the Treaty promises them.

France's problem is precisely to find outlets for its surplus agricultural and dairy products. Germany's problem, like that of Britain, has been to protect its farmers. It does so by large subsidies, and the Bonn Government has been extremely reluctant for political reasons within Germany to comply with the common policy on agriculture so painfully agreed to after much humming and hawing. Also, it has been anxious not to endanger its trading links with countries outside the Six like Denmark, from which in 1960 it imported twenty times as much live cattle as it did from France.

But even in agriculture the nations are beginning to fall into line. Tariffs on "non-liberated" products, i.e. some meats, fish, fruit and vegetables, including potatoes, processed foods and preserves had been cut by a total of 25 per cent at the beginning of 1961. Import quotas had been enlarged in some cases by as much as 20 per cent and for many products not subject to long-term contracts quotas were fixed at 30 per cent above the average level of imports during the period 1955-57.

As the Community has developed, so the rôle of the Commission has acquired greater importance. It has two horses to ride at once—the Council of Ministers and the Assembly of 142 Parliamentarians drawn from the Six countries. Apart from running the community on a day-to-day basis, it acts as watchdog for the Community and supervisor of the Treaty. Where individual enterprises, and, indeed, in some cases, Governments, have turned a blind eye to violations of the Treaty, the transgressor has been brought sharply to heel by a reminder from the Commission. Its team of inspectors keeps a watchful eye on would-be delinquents. Where necessary it has had recourse to the Court of Justice to get its way. One of the most delicate and controversial tasks of the Commission is to decide when concentrations and mergers are conducive to efficiency and therefore justified under the Treaty and when they are likely to lead to the monopolies, cartels and "dominant positions" condemned by the Treaty. In such cases, the Commission calls on the combined wisdom and discretion of its nine members. Their decisions are open to appeal.

The Commission has often been at loggerheads with the Council of Ministers on the political future of Europe. By and large the Commission favours a federal structure for the Community. The political aims of the Treaty of Rome are implicit. But those who signed the Treaty or inspired it were mainly Federalists. They saw the Economic Community as a first step towards a federated United States of Europe. Since then this principle has come under heavy fire from the "Confederalists", particularly in France, backed to some extent by the Germans. Both of these countries, understandably perhaps, see themselves as the guiding lights and major partners in the alliance—a rôle which, equally understandably, the Italians, the Dutch and the Belgians have frowned upon.

General de Gaulle's "Europe des patries" obviously has no place in a Federated Europe. But the "Federalists" are working on the assumption that the federal idea will outlive the General and his fellow "confederalists" in the Six and that Federation will emerge logically and inevitably from the close economic and cultural ties now being forged willy-nilly by the Economic Community.

This argument received considerable support at the meeting of Heads of Government of the Six held in Bonn in July, 1961, when the French discreetly played down their original demands for a Political Secretariat whose work might have fitted in well with the idea of a Confederal Europe.

Instead, a decision of some historic importance was taken. The Six set up a Commission to report on the constitutional—and institutional—forms which the new Europe might take in furtherance of the political unity which all agreed was the ultimate aim of the Six. Its terms of reference were vague but there was no mistaking that the Six had taken a decisive step towards political unification—perhaps in the direction of Federation—since any proposals submitted by the Commission and agreed upon by the Six Governments would have to be put into treaty form and would require ratification by the respective Parliaments. The Commission's proposals were expected to be ready by about the end of 1961.

The Six have constantly stressed the fact that they are an "outward-looking" Community, with no desire to be exclusive beyond wanting to keep their opponents or luke-warm supporters of unity out.

The Commission, acting for the Community, maintains friendly relations with other existing European and world organisations and many Governments are directly represented at its Brussels Headquarters. It negotiates on behalf of the Community with the GATT powers for example, and with the new OECD (Organisation for Economic Co-operation and Development). It negotiated the Agreement associating Greece with the Community. Once the Greek economy, particularly agriculture, has been strengthened by technical and financial assistance from the Commission the assumption is that Greece will become a full member of the Community.

The Agreement was negotiated mainly as a political move to draw Greece away from tempting Soviet offers of long-term credits which in the end might have sucked her into the Soviet orbit. Neither the Six nor NATO could entertain the prospect of Greece, with her smouldering Marxist sympathies, slowly disappearing behind the Communist curtain. Already by 1959 her trade with the East European bloc, including the USSR, had risen to 18 per cent of her total foreign trade.

The Agreement operates in Greece's favour in the early stages since a loan of $125 million has given an immediate boost to her economy and the Six are making efforts to increase their imports of Greek tobacco, citrus fruits and raisins all of which compete with their own products, whereas prospects of increased exports by the Six to Greece will not be good for some years to come.

Strongly backed by the Council and particularly by France, it is also taking a keen interest in Africa where the wind of change is blowing in all directions. The Commission's hope is that the wind will blow in the direction of Europe and continue to do so despite attempts by Moscow to divert it.

Thirty-six countries in Africa, 26 linked with Europe and 10 Commonwealth territories, are in the throes of independence or near-independence. They must all find assured markets for their produce. Traditionally nearly all their trade has been with Europe. It is the Commission's intention that this should remain so, whatever blocs and alignments emerge within the next decade. Some former British colonies like Ghana and, to a lesser extent, Nigeria and Sierra Leone are apprehensive lest the former French territories on their borders should enjoy preferential treatment for their exports by being associated with the Common Market. Ghana and

Nigeria dislike Common Market discrimination against their cocoa; Kenya, Uganda and Tanganyika against their coffee.

There is a strong feeling in Africa that the economic divisions in Europe must not be reproduced on that Continent.

The Commission feels that Europe provides a natural outlet for African produce.

Professor Walter Hallstein, the President of the Commission, is an active pro-African. He has suggested that the EEC might start by reducing its external tariff for Africa's principal tropical products. On coffee, for instance, the tariff might be lowered from 16 per cent to 8 per cent and any loss in preferences compensated in some other way, perhaps by direct aid payments.

Guarantee and stabilisation funds might also be set up to maintain prices. When raw material prices, for instance, were falling, the Community would make payments into these funds, whereas when prices rose sharply, the producer countries might contribute part of their increased revenue to the funds.

Professor Hallstein also feels that the Overseas Development Fund should be allowed to make loans as well as grants-in-aid. It should also be able to make loan guarantees through which African states could enjoy lower rates of interest on loans obtained outside the EEC. The Six propose to spend $1,100 million on direct aid for Africa between 1962 and 1967.

The Commission is as anxious as the United States to see that the new Africa is not lured into the Soviet orbit by spurious offers of aid whose political strings are not immediately visible to men temporarily blinded by anti-Colonialism.

A bloc which would like to set its face against the West and seek favour with Moscow has already been formed. It is the "Casablanca" bloc composed of the United Arab Republic, Morocco, Ghana, Guinea, Mali and the "Provisional Government of the Algerian Republic" based on Tunis.

It has decided to form a Common Market of its own beginning in January, 1962.

Dr. Kwame Nkrumah, the President of Ghana, is one of its leading lights. He was in Moscow in July, 1961, in search of political friendships and trade outlets. He found them both. He explained to the Soviet leaders that "Colonialism" had wrought havoc in Africa and that, had it not been for Soviet support, "the African liberation movement would have suffered the most brutal persecution". Ghana, however, had risen against the twin evils of "Colonialism" and "Imperialism" and had "crushed them both".

The Soviet leaders expressed their sympathy with Africa and explained that they too had had to fight "anti-Colonialist wars" in Europe after the 1939-45 war, particularly in Poland, Czechoslovakia and Rumania, and that only their grim determination in battle had enabled them to survive the last major Imperialist onslaught at Budapest in 1956. Understandably, President Nkrumah returned to Africa well content with the results of his visit to the Soviet Union.

Another more comprehensive bloc, known as the "Monrovia" group of 20 independent countries, has decided to set up a Customs Union with a common external tariff and has called for co-operation in building a network of roads and other communications to cover the whole territory of the group, and generally to reduce language and other cultural barriers.

This crystallisation of alliances and blocs in Africa, however provisional, may simplify the work of European agencies entrusted with the task of distributing aid to Africa.

The Western nations have great responsibilities in this field. They can only discharge them if they pool their efforts in a comprehensive and forward-looking programme of development based on the ageless skills and imaginative vigour of their peoples. Nothing could be more damaging to the Western cause than competition in aid to Africa.

The Commission has sought to strengthen its rôle of shepherd and pilot for the Community by taking into its counsel the other organs set up by the Treaty of Rome, particularly the Assembly, even where this has not been strictly necessary according to the terms of the Treaty.

It has often used the Assembly as a counter-weight to the Council of Ministers. It can usually rely on greater sympathy and support for its ultimate objectives from the Assembly than from the Council.

It has backed the suggestion, made in the Assembly, that the Executive organs of the three Communities, the European Commission, the High Authority of the Coal and Steel Community and the Euratom Commission, should be merged, since the three Communities already share three organisations in common, i.e. the Assembly, the Council of Ministers and the Court of Justice.

It can also look to America for support. There is a basic sympathy in the USA with the aims and purposes of the Community. The USA, itself an excellent example of federalism at work, sees the Commission as a permanent European institution, dedicated to the principle of unity through a Federal Europe. Indeed, supporters of federalism both in America and in Europe see in the Commission the nucleus of a European Government in its own right working in close consultation and harmony with the European Assembly of the Six, often acting as a spur and sometimes as a brake to individual Governments.

And, although it is true that the USA has at times been perturbed by the fact that the Customs Union of the Six might unduly discriminate against American trade with Europe, the need to build up Europe against the Communist régimes on its doorstep has always over-ridden these apprehensions.

But America's stake in Europe is not merely political. American direct investment capital (as opposed to portfolio or shareholdings) has been flowing into continental Europe at a greater rate since 1958 than it has into Britain. There is still today slightly more American capital in Britain than there is in the Six, owing to a large increase in investments between 1950 and 1958. But there is no denying the trend. The bigger Continental market where barriers to trade are being progressively lowered is more attractive than the smaller United Kingdom market.

Indeed, vastly increased direct British investments in the Common Market since 1958, when the Rome Treaty came into force, underline this trend. In 1959 alone, the latest year for which figures are available, the amount was £15,600,000 excluding investments by the oil and the insurance companies. Clearly, industrialists who must plan far ahead, cannot wait indefinitely for governments and politicians to "heal splits" and "close gaps".

But not only has the rapid growth of industry attracted large-scale foreign investments, rationalisation through mergers and take-overs has produced some giants in the industrial world. August Thyssen and Krupp need no introduction.

The Krupp empire, of course, was never really broken up for the simple reason that the Allies never found a buyer for the pieces. It has since been rebuilt, almost from scratch, by the discreet and patient Alfred Krupp after the Allies released him from jail. Today, its reputation for efficiency is as high as ever. It is the nearest thing to a non-profit-making organisation to be found anywhere among private enterprise in Europe, a far cry from the Nazi days.

Siemens has become the largest electrical engineering firm in the world after General Electric of America. It employs about 220,000 workers. It would welcome competition from new arrivals in EEC.

The French "Compagnie des Ateliers et Forges de la Loire" is a formidable competitor in steel. It was formed in 1953 (after the ECSC had started operating) from the merger of four steel companies, one at St. Chamond, one at St. Etienne and two at Firminy, in South-East France.

Two groups dominate the French chemical industry where considerable concentration was needed and has taken place in order to face increased competition. They are the Rhône-Poulenc-Celtex group and the Pechiney-Saint-Gobain. Both groups manufacture chemicals and synthetic textiles (including nylon), and now rival in size, if not quite ICI, or Montecatini, certainly any one of the German giants, Badische, Bayer or Hoechst.

Commercial tie-ups between French and Belgian firms and between Belgian and Dutch firms have been particularly noticeable in chain-stores and "super-markets".

In some cases private planning between firms under the auspices of the Commission, or the High Authority, has been in advance of official thinking. French and German steel interests, for instance, have agreed that they should harmonise their future investment plans so as to avoid duplication of effort and excess capacity.

The major European motor-car manufacturers may well follow suit. The Commission has already suggested that they should try to avoid cut-throat competition by co-ordinating their investment programmes in order to avoid surplus capacity.

It is impossible for the outsider to journey through the length and breadth of the Common Market countries without becoming acutely aware that the physical dismantling of political frontiers has led to the steady removal of spiritual barriers between peoples who, only a generation ago, were locked in bitter strife.

Speed of communication on land and in the air, direct

radio and TV links, freedom to travel, to trade, to study, to work in any of the countries of the Six, all these things have led the peoples of the Community to feel that Western Europe is at last beginning to achieve that unity which for centuries has eluded it.

More than any other institution of the Common Market, the Commission, with increasing support from the Assembly, is there to defend that unity. It may be more federal than the Council of Ministers in its approach to the political organisation of Europe but it is at least in agreement with the Council on the need, (a) to defend the Community against those who would see it fail, and (b) to impress upon prospective candidates that they need not apply for membership if they do not genuinely intend to obey the rules of the club and respect the spirit of the Treaty of Rome.

It is because she was loath to accept the rules of the club that Britain so long delayed any approaches to the Community and indeed sought unsuccessfully, first to widen it, then to hem it in as we shall see in the next chapter.

Chapter Four

BRITAIN AND EUROPEAN UNITY

By the end of the Second World War there was hardly a person alive who had not heard of the fabulous Churchill. The fame of Britain's wartime leader had spread to the four corners of the earth. Every Briton was, in a way, basking in the great man's glory.

The name of Britain stood as high as any country's had done in the history of mankind. Europe instinctively turned to the British Isles for leadership in the staggering task of reconstruction. Undaunted by previous failures, Europe sought a durable peace, a peace built on the time-honoured principles of freedom, democracy and justice. And who better to lead the way than a victorious Britain with Churchill, if not still in power, at least on the bridge keeping a skilled and watchful eye on the man at the helm?

Clement Richard Attlee was not of the same ilk. Churchill had been steeped in eloquence and grandeur, Attlee in Socialism and anonymity. The broad sweep of history, the grand design, were not for the Chairman of Committees.

In 1931 Attlee took over the deputy leadership of a defeated and humiliated party. In 1945 he found himself the leader of a victorious, buoyant Party ready and eager to bring the Socialist millenium to Britain, the millenium of Keir Hardie, not of Karl Marx.

British Socialism, essentially Noncomformist, was not for export. The Labour Party, as the Government of Britain, could and did co-operate with other European Governments which derived their power from the Catholic parties of the Centre. But these parties themselves were basically as suspect as the orthodox Marxist parties of the Left. There might be collaboration in certain limited fields of reconstruction but there could be no true community of spirit or action for the future. In any case Labour was far too busy, at Westminster, rushing through legislation the need for which had, apparently, accumulated over the years.

Europe would therefore be kept at arm's length, the only concession being made to the French in the shape of the Dunkirk Treaty, negotiated and signed while victory was still warm. It was in a mood of triumph and virtuous isolation that the leaders of the new Europe found the Attlees and the Daltons, the Morrisons and the Bevins—the leaders of the new Britain.

In 1950, an historic year this, M. Robert Schuman, French Foreign Minister at the time, launched the first of the schemes for the unification of Europe—the European Coal and Steel Community. This was to be essentially a supranational organisation because it was basic to the concept of the new Europe that individual countries should no longer have unlimited control over raw materials which are as much the sinews of war as of peace.

It was precisely this supranational quality of the "Schuman Plan", as it was called at the time, that disqualified it in the eyes of the British Labour Government, and, it must be said in all truthfulness, of the Conservatives who were in opposition at the time.

Moreover, the French approaches were made at a time when the shine was wearing off Labour's victory and the party was in no mood for ventures abroad, particularly as events in Korea were beginning to cast their shadows over Europe. The Labour Government sensed rightly that the country as a whole disliked the idea of participation in supranational organisations. Labour, as a party, would turn it down as a matter of political principle. Socialist doctrine required that the basic means of production should be in the hands of the Government and that certainly meant coal, iron and steel. The Federalists and supporters of World Government who might have been in favour of going in were insignificant in numbers.

The Conservatives would have no truck with it for the more traditional reason that it meant abandoning national sovereignty to a foreign organisation led by political theorists assumed at the time to have their heads in the clouds—not a prospect likely to appeal to any good Conservative in 1950.

Conservative leaders, while they were in opposition, spoke eloquently of unity—for others. At Zürich Churchill had invited France to "take Germany by the hand" and lead her back into the community of European nations. At Fulton, Missouri, he had suggested that America should join with Europe in defence of Western civilisation.

At no time did they suggest that Britain should herself take the lead in Europe by joining supranational organisations which might lead to a federation or confederation of European states.

Much lip-service was paid to European unity by members of the "United Europe Movement" founded by Churchill himself. But, basically, the Conservatives were in agreement with Labour on the need to steer clear of anything which might smack of Federalism or a surrender of sovereignty.

Indeed, Conservatives derived some secret pleasure from the fact that it fell to Labour to reject the first concrete proposal by the French that Britain should join the supranational Coal and Steel Pool. They chided the Labour Government on the rather brutal, doctrinaire, way in which they spurned M. Schuman's overtures, but had they been in power they too would have rejected them only possibly with rather more elegance.

There is no doubt that, in turning down the invitation

to join the Schuman Plan in 1950, the Labour Government, although it was on its way out at the time, spoke for the whole of Britain.

It is still one of the mysteries of French diplomacy that the approaches to Britain to join supranational organisations in Europe were so clumsy. The ascetic Spartan-living Robert Schuman was of an Aristotelian cast of mind. Like so many Europeans, he saw the future organisation of Europe as a political pyramid, minutely planned and meticulously built—the very antithesis of the pragmatic English approach to European institutions, based as it was, and largely still is, on the formula of "close association" with few specific commitments—a formula which has become a mystical byword in Whitehall's dealings with the Continent.

The British donkey has on many occasions since 1945 been led to the waters of supranationalism but he has never actually drunk of them. Whether he will drink those of the Common Market has yet to be shown conclusively.

Having been politely rebuffed by the British, Robert Schuman and his European colleagues went ahead on their own, and the Steel Community was set up in 1952, in just less than a year.

The next approach to Britain to join in a European pooling of sovereignty was M. Pflimlin's ill-fated "Agricultural Pool" or "Pool vert", as the French called it. The least said about this plan the better. It was altogether too premature. After that came the approach to join the ill-starred European Defence Community which the French National Assembly eventually turned down after teams of officials in Whitehall under Sir Anthony Eden's guidance had burnt the midnight oil working out a satisfactory form of association for Britain.

Meanwhile, of course, all British Governments had been happy to take an active part in European organisations where co-operation was on a Government-to-

Government basis and all important decisions were taken unanimously. Such organisations were NATO, the OEEC (Organisation for European Economic Co-operation) and its subsidiary, the European Payments Union. The Council of Europe which sits in Strasbourg and Western European Union with headquarters in Brussels were other organisations where co-operation was at Government level.

But in the eyes of MM. Monnet, Schuman, Spaak, Hallstein and Adenauer, the OEEC could never possibly be a substitute for the European Economic Community. It had been set up to distribute Marshall Aid, not to frame the economic future of Europe. But the days of the OEEC were in any case numbered and indeed it has now been replaced by the Organisation for Economic Co-operation and Development which includes the USA and Canada.

Meanwhile, West Germany was emerging as one of the major economic powers in Europe and because of this economic strength would obviously in time, through NATO, become one of the major military powers as well.

The attempt to strap West Germany firmly to Western Europe through the European Defence Community had failed miserably. Nothing daunted, however, the planners went into conference first at Messina then at Venice, and although proceedings were held up for some time owing to the tensions created in Europe by the Suez affair and the uprising in Budapest, the Treaty of Rome was signed on March 25, 1957, by the same powers which had come together in the Coal and Steel Pool—France, West Germany, Italy, Holland, Belgium and Luxembourg.

Thus another floor had been added to the European edifice. Even the flagpole was in position. But under what colours would the three Communities eventually sail? Federation or Confederation?

The matter has still not been decided. The debate

goes on in the assemblies and seminars of Europe and is likely to become even more controversial now that Britain has decided to apply for membership.

But at the time, 1956-57, there was no likelihood of Britain's moving into any of the floors of the new building, nor was she invited to do so.

With M. Schuman's bitter experience behind them, and with no visible change of mood in Britain, the Six went ahead by themselves. They did not rule out the idea of closer links between themselves and the other members of the OEEC once the Treaty of Rome had been signed, but there was no great enthusiasm for the British suggestion that the Six should actually join a Free Trade Area, in which the other members of OEEC would get the benefit of the tariff reductions to be brought about by the Six while accepting none of the obligations the latter had accepted under the Treaty of Rome. This looked suspiciously as if "perfidious Albion" was up to her tricks again, trying to get the best of both worlds, or alternatively, trying to kill the Common Market by pressure from outside.

The Six which had just taken the plunge into the very deep waters of European integration were in no mood to make life even more difficult for themselves. Here was an experiment, unique in history, which would be difficult enough to work at the best of times, leave alone taking on Britain and her Free Trade Area partners on terms which would be wholly favourable to the latter. Britain had stipulated all along that Agriculture was to be left out of the Free Trade Area. As France had agricultural surpluses to dispose of, she saw no reason why tariff reductions should apply to British manufactured goods entering France and not to France's foodstuffs entering Britain.

Negotiations dragged on unsuccessfully and half-heartedly through 1957 and part of 1958. The Inter-Governmental Committee of OEEC, formed under the

Chairmanship of Mr. Reginald Maudling, British Paymaster-General at the time, got bogged down in the consideration of a mass of special rules and exceptions which might after all apply to agriculture, and much time was lost in the futile examination of a possible system of certificates of origin. This was important because, as the members of the proposed Free Trade Area who were not also members of the Common Market were free to deal individually and as they liked with the outside world, there was nothing to stop them re-exporting goods bought abroad to France with the minimum of reprocessing. Nor would it be easy to determine how far goods were British which had a percentage of foreign constituent bodies.

All this tiresome and at times irrelevant work was brought to an abrupt end with the advent to power in France of General de Gaulle.

The General's knowledge of the fine points of economics, like Churchill's, was limited. But he had the sagacity to retain the services of one expert in particular. That expert was M. Olivier Wormser, Head of the Economic Department of the French Foreign Office. M. Wormser, like Professor Walter Hallstein, Chairman of the European Commission, was a firm believer in the principle that Britain could either come into the Common Market or she could stay out. All France and her partners in EEC asked was that if she came in she should not try to wreck the organisation. If she stayed out, she should not try to kill it by other means. For the Free Trade Area, so fondly canvassed by the British, he had no use whatsoever. It was an ill-conceived device whereby Britain in particular sought to join the tariff-lowering band-wagon on easy terms. He had no difficulty in convincing General de Gaulle that a firm hand was needed with the British. On November 14, 1958, the General's new Foreign Minister, M. Couve de Murville, issued a statement to the Press which fell like a bomb on

Mr. Maudling's Inter-Governmental Committee. It stated simply that it did not seem possible to establish the Free Trade Area proposed by Britain and that a new solution would have to be found.

From that moment on the Free Trade Area idea was dead. It was never to be revived. Smarting under the French rebuff, the British Government set about establishing a rival organisation known as the European Free Trade Association (EFTA). This association grouped together most of the countries in OEEC which, like Britain, had no great liking for the tight economic links the Six had forged between themselves and which looked like leading to a Federation or Confederation of States in which a large measure of sovereignty would be surrendered to supranational institutions. They were Britain, Norway, Sweden, Denmark, Austria, Switzerland and Portugal. They became known as the "Outer Seven" as opposed to the inner "Six" of the Common Market.

The EFTA was negotiated in 1959 and signed in Stockholm in January, 1960. It set up shop at Geneva. The Seven set out to reduce tariffs between themselves by stages roughly corresponding to those adopted by the Common Market. But there would be no common external tariff. Each country would be free to negotiate its own tariffs with the outside world. And although there was to be an attempt to harmonise trade policies and generally live together in peace and understanding, nothing like the overall planning and control of the Common Market was envisaged.

EFTA, of course, was no substitute for genuine all-round free trade in Europe. In population and size of markets, it was lop-sided. Britain provided 51 million of the 89 million population and provided by far the largest single market. EFTA countries only took 10 per cent of her exports. As the major industrial power in the group she would naturally look for a sizeable increase in exports of manufactured goods. But the Swedes and the Swiss are also large manufacturers, and Danish food imports into Britain fight a running battle with home and Commonwealth produce. Every time food imported into Britain from Europe benefits from some tariff or quantity concession, farmers in Britain are up in arms, and so, to a lesser extent, are Commonwealth producers. The same goes for pulp and timber.

The basic fault of the EFTA was that its economies were not complementary. Nations cannot prosper by taking in one another's washing!

As a means of bringing the Common Market to heel, it failed utterly. The Common Market countries had their Treaty of Rome to stick to, the negotiation of which had been difficult enough. No member of the Six would agree to derogations of the Treaty which would mean, in effect, renegotiating it.

The EFTA countries, in the early stages, put on a brave front, and tariffs were lowered in harmony with the reductions made by the Six, but by the autumn of 1960 it had become clear that the organisation was breaking up because its leading member, Britain, had decided that the time had come to switch from EFTA to the Common Market, however painful the transfer might be. The reasons for Britain's wanting to join the Common Market are indeed cogent. They are set forth in the following chapter.

Chapter Five

APPLICATION FOR MEMBERSHIP

WHEN the Treaty setting up the Common Market was signed in Rome in March, 1957, few people in Britain and, indeed, few members of the British Government, gave it much of a chance. It had taken two years to negotiate, two years in which to reconcile, perhaps only on paper, widely divergent and often conflicting interests. Two of its members, France and Italy, were suffering from acute political instability. The Benelux countries were lesser members. Only Germany seemed to be pursuing a steady disciplined course with the imperturbable, rock-like Dr. Adenauer at the helm. There was even the possibility that the Treaty might not be ratified in one, or maybe two, countries. The French National Assembly had thrown out the European Defence Community in 1954 with a comfortable majority. The Coal and Steel Community was not necessarily a guide. Five of its members, France, Italy and the three Benelux countries, had seen the undoubted wisdom of preventing independent expansion by the infamous Ruhr industries and were prepared to give this first instalment of the Monnet/Schuman experiment a trial. But the new Community, the Economic Community, was a very different kettle of fish. It might not be as supranational as the Coal and Steel Pool, and indeed is not, but it contained a far larger dose of voluntary integration. This integration would seep through to the roots of economic life. It would spill over into the field of politics.

And, politically, the Six were far from united, with differing views on Communism, East-West relations, Berlin, the Eastern frontiers of Germany, Disarmament, the United Nations, Africa. Even NATO was not immune, at the time, from the cross-fire of politicians with both eyes fixed on the electorate.

There was not the remotest chance of Britain's becoming a member. Indeed, she was not even invited to do so. This was 1955. By 1961 she was applying for membership of her own accord. What had happened in the intervening five years? Little short of a revolution in the foreign policy of Britain.

Two Ministers were in charge in the early stages of the Cabinet's relations with the Six. They were Sir David Eccles, President of the Board of Trade at the time, and Mr. Reginald Maudling, Paymaster-General, and subsequently President of the Board of Trade. Neither had much faith in the ability of the Six to coalesce, to sink their differences in what looked like a grandiose scheme for squaring the circle, i.e. for uniting countries whose history and background were so dissimilar as to rule out any possibility of their coming together in a permanent embrace.

One of two things could happen to the Common Market countries. They could either make a go of the Treaty of Rome or they could allow it to become a deadletter, according to the political set-up of the day.

Sir David and Mr. Maudling, with the help of their professional advisers in Whitehall, had little difficulty in persuading their Cabinet colleagues that the best policy at the outset was to sit tight and "wait and see". There was the firm conviction in many Ministerial quarters that if the Six were given enough rope, they would hang themselves. The Economic Community was quite impossible, an aberration! The hard-headed businessmen and bankers of the Continent would soon put an end to the pipe-dreams of the Monnets and the Schumans, the Spaaks and the Hallsteins. When the planners of the Six came down to earth, they would have the wool torn from their eyes by the harsh facts of life. When this happened, one big heave by Britain and the EEC would be over the cliff.

But it didn't happen this way. The planners were tough men. They were not to be deflected from their course by the hostility of a nation still clinging to the "balance of power" as a means of preventing the resurgence of Europe in one united bloc. The will to unity in Europe was dismally underrated by men unable to appreciate the profound changes which were taking place in the minds and habits of peoples whose lives had been shattered by the experiences of two world wars in one generation.

This misreading of events on the Continent persisted right up to the formation of the European Free Trade Association (EFTA). EFTA, in the minds of its British sponsors, was never intended to be an end in itself, and understandably so for the reasons already stated. What it was intended to do was force the Six into an association with the Seven which would go some way to preventing the permanent division of Europe into two rival economic blocs.

But the Common Market countries stood their ground. They saw no future in an association which would bring tariff benefits to the Seven without committing the Seven to any of the far-reaching economic and quasi-political clauses of the Treaty of Rome.

By the autumn of 1960 the truth had begun to dawn in Whitehall and by the spring of 1961 it had percolated through to London's specialist Press. Britain was fast losing the battle with the Common Market. Far from collapsing or giving way under pressure from the Seven, the Six looked healthier than ever. They had survived the entry on to the stage of General de Gaulle. Indeed, ironically enough, it was the new, astute and enigmatic master of France who helped them to bring the British to Canossa, or rather to Brussels where the final act of surrender would be performed.

Professor Erhard, the German President at the time, of the Council of Ministers, who received the British application for full membership, called it an "historic document" and August 10, 1961, an historic date. And indeed they were. But what did the British communication mean? Did it mean that the British Government had finally, in one dramatic gesture, jettisoned the policy of the "balance of power", a policy which had served British interests so well since the days of Marlborough? Or did it mean that the cunning English were up to their tricks again, trying to wreck the EEC from within, an "inside job" as it were?

Suspicions of British motives die hard on the Continent. Not all the Governments of the Six or all members of the Commission could express unreserved pleasure at seeing the British apply to join the Club. Admitting the British might mean weakening the structure of the Community and creating new political problems, while the Six were patiently trying to solve old ones. Had not *The Sunday Times*, in a leading article in the spring of 1961, said that if Britain joined the Common Market one of her aims would be to prevent it from setting itself up as a "Third Force" in the world, or from becoming "anti-American" or "anti-Soviet". *The Sunday Times* does not represent official opinion in Britain, but most foreign observers thought that in this particular instance its views were sufficiently close to those of Whitehall for the Governments of the Six to sit up and take note. Indeed, the Prime Minister himself said later, "We can lead better from within."

In the debate in the House of Commons, which followed the Prime Minister's announcement, many speakers had suggested that the application should be hedged round with a number of demands for guarantees that British interests would be protected. Others had suggested that Britain should state then and there that if she entered she in no way committed herself to any form of political integration. Mr. Edward Heath, the Lord Privy Seal, speaking for the Government, had emphasised that all the Treaty of Rome called for was economic integration and that was all Britain would be agreeing to. Sir Lionel Heald, Q.C., M.P., a former Attorney-General, had suggested wrongly in *The Times* that Article 237 of the Treaty of Rome could be used to modify the substance of the Treaty in such a way as to allay all Britain's fears about the Commonwealth and Agriculture. The net effect of these opinions was to strengthen the impression that Britain was joining for a wide variety of reasons and might be a very awkward member. At all events, the Council and Commission of the Common Market took the charitable view of Britain's motives and gave a very warm welcome to Mr. Macmillan's announcement and to his assurances that if Britain went in, she would "go in honestly, to strengthen the Community and to contribute to its success".

When it had become obvious that the attempt to link EEC and EFTA had failed, the Government had been left with the clear choice—to join or not to join the EEC? Not to join meant to become progressively more isolated not only from the economic life of the Continent but from its political life, since the tendency was for the Six to co-ordinate their political activities and foreign policies more and more closely, to the exclusion of Britain.

It meant that Britain would be forced back on to the Commonwealth as her main source of prosperity and power. In her isolation from the main current of European events, Britain would no longer be able to count on American support. She would no longer enjoy the special relationships which, in the days of Churchill, and even to some extent, in the days of Sir Stafford Cripps, had marked her out as a special and reliable ally of the United States. For reasons which are explained fully in the following pages, Britain shied away from this course. On the other hand, to join meant that Britain recognised the inevitability of change and would not "drop out of the main stream of the world's life" as the Prime Minister put it in the House of Commons on August 2, 1961.

Negotiations for Britain's membership of the European Communities started in November, 1961 after some early skirmishing between the Commission and the Council of Ministers had shown that the Commission was likely to adopt a tougher line on the conditions of entry than was the Council of Ministers.

Professor Walter Hallstein, the President of the Commission, wanted Britain to produce a "shopping list" at the start of the negotiations—or even before—whereas the Council of Ministers decided that a preliminary run over the course was not necessary. In the event, the Commission did not become the sole negotiating body and was given an advisory rôle more in keeping with Article 237 of the Treaty and with the importance of the occasion.

The importance of the occasion was not lost on the British Government which appointed a very high-powered team to do the negotiating under the general supervision of Mr. Edward Heath, the Lord Privy Seal and Cabinet Minister in charge of the negotiations. The team is led by Sir Pierson Dixon, Britain's Ambassador in Paris. He has under him 6 very senior civil servants from Whitehall. They are: Mr. Eric Roll, Deputy Head of the Delegation and a Deputy Secretary in the Ministry of Agriculture, Fisheries and Food; Sir Roderick Barclay, a former British Ambassador to Denmark, representing the Foreign Office; Mr. G. R. Bell of the Treasury; Sir Henry Lintott of the Commonwealth Relations Office; Sir William Gorell-Barnes of the Colonial Office and Mr. G. H. Andrews of the Board of Trade.

The negotiations will be delicate, complex and protracted because of the large number of interests to be reconciled not only in Britain but in the Commonwealth. The conference of Finance Ministers of the Commonwealth held at Accra, Ghana, in September, 1961, showed how resolute the Commonwealth countries could be in defence of their own interests. In Britain, the Commonwealth Industries Association, The Anti-Common Market League and all those who oppose Britain's entry on a variety of grounds, are by no means a spent force. The Government will need strong nerves if it is to see this matter through to the bitter end. The anti-Common Marketeers are waiting in the wings to strike— if and when they get the opportunity. If the negotiations run into heavy weather and deadlock is threatened, the Government may find itself attacked from unexpected quarters. Not all Cabinet Ministers are as enthusiastically in favour of joining as are say, Mr. Peter Thorneycroft, Mr. Duncan Sandys, or indeed, Mr. Heath. Lukewarm supporters of participation know they are on a good wicket because, on the face of it, they have most of the Commonwealth on their side.

If they make enough noise on the sidelines at the right moment, they may well make deadlock permanent. If they are given just a few concrete facts to go on concerning the negotiations—either through leaks to the Press or through contacts with Commonwealth observers at the talks, they could do untold damage. They would inevitably get a distorted picture of the bargaining and would be able to mislead public opinion in support of their arguments for non-entry.

A reasonable forecast of the length of the negotiations is one year. Some optimists speak of Britain's acceding to the Treaty of Rome by the end of 1962. Time will show.

Chapter Six

THE REASONS FOR JOINING

In reaching their momentous decision to apply for membership, the Government naturally looked at the problem from every conceivable angle, political, economic, historic, emotional. They had to consider what the effects of joining or not joining would be on industry, on finance, on the Trade Unions, on wages and prices, on social conditions, on agriculture, on defence, on sovereignty, on foreign policy, on the Commonwealth, on relations with America and on the life and habits generally of a people so deeply rooted in an island soil that insularity over the centuries had become a creed, and to be English, or Scottish, or Welsh, or Irish was to be a cut above the average mortal. Indeed, when the author asked the Head of an Education Department in one of the Home Counties whether he favoured the Common Market, he replied indignantly, "Certainly not! The only time we've ever been into Europe has been to knock their heads together."

Bearing in mind the virtues of tradition and the evils of prejudice, let us look in turn at each of the problems that faced the Government, taking the Commonwealth first because of the profound impact membership of EEC would have on that unique institution.

In 1947 the word "Empire" was struck out of the official vocabulary. It lingered on mainly in the Beaverbrook Press. Since then the Commonwealth has acquired a mystique and romance all its own. It has come to be regarded with the reverence normally reserved for the Monarchy, Shakespeare or the Bank of England. Yet few people have in their minds a clear picture of the facts which rule the Commonwealth.

It is perfectly true that the Commonwealth is unique in the sense that all its members are completely independent, that the Republican members (India, Pakistan and Ghana) recognise the Queen as "Head of the Commonwealth" (whatever that curious juridical formula may mean), that the bonds that unite appear to be more powerful than the strains that divide, that these bonds have no formal shape, that they are tighter where the same races meet, and looser where the races part, that they are often intangible but very much in evidence in periods of crisis. In short, most Englishmen like to think of the Commonwealth as something peculiarly English, something that mercifully defies the logic of the Continentals, a multi-racial grouping of nations which has proved a natural and worthy successor to the old Empire, in fact a unique answer to the claims of nationalism in all the territories once ruled by the British Raj.

But there is another side to the picture. The Commonwealth is still, of course, unique. But there are strains and centrifugal forces which are weakening it. The older members like Canada, Australia and New Zealand long ago reached maturity. They have world problems of their own to face which force them to look outwards, towards the USA, Japan, China rather than inwards towards the United Kingdom. During the first half of the century all three relied for their defence on the Royal Navy. Today all three look to America for protection; Canada because she is an American power; Australia and New Zealand because they are Pacific powers (ANZUS pact).

Economically, except in the case of New Zealand, the United Kingdom market is no longer vitally essential. Canada's trade with the USA is vastly more important than her trade with Britain, Australia's trade with the United Kingdom is diminishing because she is looking for and has found other markets nearer to hand, in South-East Asia for instance, where transport costs are smaller. Australia's industrialisation is opening up new vistas for her in the whole of Asia. One of Australia's problems is how to increase her population. Economic expansion which means industrial development is one of the surest ways.

The newer members, such as India, Pakistan and Ceylon, have problems which are quite distinct from those of the United Kingdom. In many cases the help of Soviet Russia and West Germany, over and above that of Britain and America, has been sought to solve them. India aims at being a net exporter of steel in ten years' time. Pakistan, despite close ties culturally with Britain and militarily with Britain and America (CENTO pact, ex-Baghdad pact), has often complained with good reason that these ties are not always beneficial to her and that the neutralism of India is more attractive and better rewarded in London and Washington than is the alliance with Pakistan. Pakistan rightly points out that American industry influences this attitude, seeing far more trading opportunities in India than in Pakistan, owing to the vastness of the population. India sees herself as the natural leader of the non-Communist states of Asia, and now considers the Persian Gulf and the Middle East as her natural markets, whereas before, these areas were essentially a United Kingdom sphere of interest.

Ceylon's ties with Britain are getting more and more tenuous as British tea planters and European oil interests have reason to know.

Malaya and Singapore have still not found their feet.

In Africa, where the winds of nationalism are blowing a Force 8 gale, former British territories now independent are staying in the Commonwealth mainly for economic reasons. There may be a latent respect for some missionaries and white farmers but there is little sentimental attachment to the English as such.

Here again, many of these new nations would not be above accepting Soviet support and aid in their efforts to reconstruct Africa on African lines. Many of their leaders are ambitious men. Now that the British are on the way out—and who can deny it?—these leaders are on a loose political rein. They seek power on an Africa-wide basis. They argue, rightly, that many of the old frontiers artificially created by the white man must go. As the former occupier, the United Kingdom will be hard put to it to hold on to such economic advantages as it enjoys in those territories which it is in the process of vacating.

The Sterling Area is still a strong financial link between the members of the Commonwealth (except Canada which is in the dollar area), but if the United Kingdom cannot keep its head above water economically, its position as head of the area and its chief banker will be in jeopardy.

The hard economic fact about the Commonwealth is that the balance of trade between the United Kingdom and the Commonwealth is tending to become unfavourable to the United Kingdom and looks like growing increasingly and permanently so. During the 10 years between 1950 and 1960 United Kingdom exports to Commonwealth countries dropped from 47 per cent to 42 per cent of the total United Kingdom exports. This was due in large part to the fact that the United Kingdom's share of each member's total imports has declined in recent years. A typical example is Australia, where manufactured imports from the United Kingdom dropped from 70 per cent of total imports in 1954 to under 50 per cent in 1960.

Canada is another case. Canadian exports to the United Kingdom far outweigh United Kingdom exports to Canada. In 1960 the United Kingdom imported nearly £380 million worth of Canadian goods and sent to Canada goods worth only £220 million. This is not wholly due to the inefficiency of United Kingdom salesmen or to faulty quality or value in United Kingdom goods! Like the United Kingdom, the older Commonwealth countries go through economic crises at varying

D

intervals. When they have balance of payments troubles, they do not hesitate to restrict imports from the United Kingdom along with imports from countries outside the Commonwealth. During 1960 British exports of cars to Canada did particularly well, too well, presumably, because the Diefenbaker Government were quite prepared, in the last resort, to clamp a 10 per cent import duty on British cars.

Another reason why United Kingdom exports are declining is that, in expanding their trade with the outside world, Commonwealth countries conclude reciprocal agreements in which, quite naturally, they offer the other party trading opportunities which inevitably hit imports from the United Kingdom. The Australian-Japanese Trade Agreement of July, 1957, is a case in point. Japan's exports of manufactured goods to Australia jumped spectacularly after the signature of this document.

The progressive industrialisation of countries like Australia and even New Zealand, India and Pakistan is inevitable. The pace will vary according to geography, but the trend is unmistakable. Ironically enough, Britain herself laid the foundations of this industrialisation by supplying much of the capital equipment and finance which is now, in a sense, being used against her. United Kingdom exports to these countries have fallen also because so many United Kingdom firms have built plant and set up shop in the Dominions, the effect of which has been to increase employment in the Dominions and reduce it in the United Kingdom. The earnings of shipping companies have also been affected by this shift in manufacturing activity.

When one considers that Britain, as a nation, lives entirely by manufacturing, exporting the bulk of its manufactures and importing virtually all its raw materials and half its food, the trend towards economic self-sufficiency and industrialisation in the Commonwealth was one of the factors which weighed most heavily in the

Government's decision not to allow itself to be deprived of a fair and expanding share of the large markets close at hand in Europe. These markets are not easy ones, but they are developing at a greater speed than those of any other group in the world. M. Jean Monnet has forecast that by 1975 production in the Common Market will have reached American levels. There is no reason to doubt his forecast.

Lord Home, the Foreign Secretary, has said that if Britain wants to remain the leading partner in the Commonwealth, and fulfil all her overseas commitments, she must earn another £500 million a year in exports. How is this to be done? It certainly cannot be done by staying out of the mainstream of European economic life and concentrating on expanding the economy of the Commonwealth, as some sections of opinion in Britain have suggested.

The idea that Britain can recover (or retain) her position as a leading world power by concentrating all her energies on developing the Commonwealth and letting Europe take care of itself is, at first sight, an attractive one and has many exponents in the United Kingdom, in-including members of all political parties and the "Commonwealth Industries Association". But it does not stand up to close analysis.

In the first place exports can only go in large quantities to countries with a high or reasonable standard of living, and, on the scale Britain produces manufactured articles, the bigger the markets the better. Numbers, i.e. consumers, count in mass production. Where are the mass markets in the present-day Commonwealth? India and Pakistan, with a total estimated population in 1961 of 500 millions plus, have the numbers but not the money. Australia, New Zealand and Canada have a high standard of living, the money but not the numbers. Between them they can only muster about 30 millions, whereas if Britain and most of the other members of

EFTA joined the Common Market, the United Kingdom would be trading in a market of nearly 270 millions.

At the moment, leaving out South Africa because she is no longer a member of the Commonwealth, the United Kingdom trades in an area of approximately 650 million inhabitants of whom barely 90 millions have any real purchasing power and of whom the United Kingdom accounts for 51 millions. The rest are made up from Canada, Australia, New Zealand and an estimated 9 millions from India, Pakistan, Ceylon, Malaya, Singapore, Nigeria, Ghana, Sierra Leone and the Federation of Rhodesia and Nyasaland (the dependent Colonial territories are not included).

It is argued that all these markets are capable of vast expansion whereas those of Western Europe are not. It is certainly true that there is room for vast expansion in the Commonwealth but will it take place on the scale and at the speed required to rescue the United Kingdom economy from its present plight? Nothing in the political and economic programmes of the Commonwealth countries suggests that it will. In the second place, it would be politically impossible to get the Commonwealth to make a combined, concerted drive to help the United Kingdom. Leadership by the United Kingdom in this matter would be restricted.

For the United Kingdom to begin to consider the Commonwealth as an alternative to Europe, the first requirement would be a vast and steady increase in population where it matters most, i.e. in Canada, Australia, New Zealand and possibly South Africa, where there is room for expansion (the population of Greater London which spreads into the Home Counties is larger than that of the whole of Australia, and the population of New Zealand is only slightly larger than that of Birmingham and Glasgow combined). Where is this increase coming from? With the best will in the world the Dominions cannot stimulate their reproduction rate beyond a certain figure. Are Britons from the United Kingdom prepared to emigrate in the numbers required to make an appreciable difference to the population and birth-rate of the Commonwealth? The emigration figures since the 1939-45 war and the experiences of emigrants suggest the contrary.

The second requirement would be that the economy of the Commonwealth as a whole should be closely co-ordinated and planned by some central organisation with power to direct investment, finance and trade policy—a sort of Commonwealth Common Market with complete free trade internally and a common external tariff. The external trade of many members has already assumed patterns which rule this out automatically.

The countries of the Commonwealth with their widely differing political, economic and cultural outlooks are no nearer a Common Market of their own than they are to having a common foreign policy or a common policy on demographic expansion. It is possible to conceive that a super-body of wise men, with absolute powers in all fields, could, if they were given time and vast sums of money, so reconstruct the Commonwealth as to make it one of the most powerful economic and therefore political blocs in the world. But it is dangerously Utopian to suggest that a reconstruction of this magnitude could be performed by sovereign Governments all of which are subject to the strains and tensions of everyday politics and see reality in their own way.

In international affairs the Commonwealth seldom acts as a bloc, nor could it be expected to do so. At the United Nations, for instance, the Asian and African members invariably support the Afro-Asian bloc (to which they contribute in any case the greatest numbers), if necessary against the United Kingdom and the Western Powers. The Suez episode split the Commonwealth from top to bottom as, of course, it split the United Kingdom. Only Australia and New Zealand gave Sir Anthony Eden any real support. Even Canada found it advantageous to support John Foster Dulles rather than the British Premier.

All in all, the Government rightly came to the conclusion that the Commonwealth could never become a suitable economic alternative to the Common Market. A detailed examination of the situation and reactions in the major Commonwealth countries supports this view to the hilt.

NEW ZEALAND

Economically, New Zealand is the most deeply involved of all the Commonwealth countries with the United Kingdom. Reports which speak of her "ruin" if no suitable arrangements are made for special treatment for her agricultural products are not alarmist. Apart from a nasty jolt in the 1930s, the pattern was traditional, Britain wanted from New Zealand all the meat and dairy produce she could get. In 1952, to encourage New Zealand to step up meat production, Britain promised unrestricted entry until 1967, the same assurance in respect of dairy produce being given in 1957.

Even before the Common Market was a reality, New Zealand, with one of the most efficient low-cost farm productions in the world, recognised that her extra production channelled to the British market was only having the effect of driving down the price against herself and sought additional markets in the United States, Europe and elsewhere.

But the United Kingdom, it was assumed, would always be the mainstay. What happens if that mainstay is removed? Actual quantities often speak louder than percentages. In 1959 New Zealand exported in all, 344,900 tons of lamb and mutton, 307,600 tons to the United Kingdom, duty-free. The Common Agricultural Policy of the EEC envisages a 20 per cent duty (plus variable import levies). This might well rule out almost the whole of the European market; New Zealand lamb is not popular on the Continent and is not, in 1961, doing well even in England. New Zealand lamb is however "innocent", i.e. harmless to the agriculture of the Six. Only France and Italy of the Six have sizeable sheep populations and together they produce less than two-thirds of the output from Britain's own sheep farms. Lamb might, justifiably, then, be the subject of special arrangements. If not, it is hard to see what will become of this trade. The New Zealand farmers, highly efficient and experienced, have economic good sense on their side and the world is crying out for food, but India with her 438 million to feed (625 million forecast by 1976) is giving exchange priority to capital imports (she has ambitions to become a net exporter of steel products within the next ten years), and other possible consumers in the Far and Middle East are also short of money. America is more interested in beef (hamburgers).

New Zealand's second major export is cheese. Of a total export of 79,400 tons, 73,900 tons went to Britain. Here again New Zealand cheese, good as it is of the "mouse-trap" variety, does not appeal to the Continental palate (Dr. Summerskill, when Parliamentary Secretary to the Ministry of Food once referred to European "frivolous cheeses"!). Duty envisaged by the Common Market is of the order of 23 per cent.

Third staple is butter. Of 154,800 tons of butter sent to 20 different countries, 142,700 tons went to Britain. Despite dumping of surpluses (Mr. Holyoake in August, 1961, named Eire, Finland, France and Poland as offenders in a protest to the U.K. Government) which have debased the price and reduced demand, New Zealand has held on to the lion's share of the butter market. Duty envisaged is 24 per cent. The United Kingdom would undoubtedly buy less at a lower price, but taking into account supplies from all sources, the housewife would be asked to pay a higher price and this might cause a decline in demand in favour of margarine. Yellow, close-textured and rather flavourless, New Zealand butter does not go well on the Continent though it might sell for cooking in France and Germany.

The last important New Zealand staple is wool. In 1960, despite poor prices, New Zealand wool sold in the United Kingdom to the value of £35·5m. Even about wool, New Zealand is alarmed. Though this would be unaffected by the Common Market, continuing to come to both the United Kingdom and the Common Market duty-free, New Zealand farmers have not been slow to point out that if you want the fleece you've got to want the animal inside it!

In return for these primary products New Zealand has received from the United Kingdom the usual export staples: In 1960, machinery £27m., cars and commercial vehicles £18½m., iron and steel £9m. and chemicals £8m. Presumably if United Kingdom preference for New Zealand products goes, so does New Zealand preference for British manufactured goods. But the market is small, New Zealand's population is only 2,400,000. There is no temptation here to the EEC to make an important exception to the principles laid down in the Treaty of Rome.

Faced with the possibility of economic disaster, New Zealand has remained calm and unembittered, recognising that if Britain's industry were to slump because she was excluded from the Common Market, she would not, in any case, be able to purchase New Zealand's primary products. The prospects of special guarantees for New Zealand's exports, if only for a limited period, will be one of the main points at issue as far as the Commonwealth is concerned when negotiations for Britain's entry begin.

Meanwhile a switch to beef seems an insurance. Beef is more acceptable in America and Europe than lamb, but there is not much time before 1967, and the best New Zealand dairy land, if turned over to beef, is said to bring only one-third of the revenue of dairy farming. Infant industries, plastics, aluminium (S. Island), pulp and paper, steel, oil refining, etc., will be hurried along and the tourist industry encouraged.

Auckland is now only 27 hours by air from London, 22 from New York. In the past 10 years the number of visitors and receipts have roughly trebled (nearly £3·8m. in 1960). New Zealand has a climate so temperate that livestock winter in the open and boasts some of the most "fabulous" scenery in the world, countless lakes and fjords, superb beaches, the snowy slopes of the Southern Alps, the hot springs, the glow-worm caves, the Maori civilisation, hunting, sailing and fishing—all unspoiled. Enormous expansion is possible, but is limited at present by shortage of accommodation. However, New Zealand has pioneered the erection of mobile prefabricated houses, mostly wooden, on a large scale. While full-scale hotels are awaited, chalet development might be the answer. Capital is needed but the Reserve Bank is offering very special facilities to investors.

Coupled with her economic fears go doubts as to whether Britain, ever more deeply involved in Europe, will have time, and energy to devote to her Commonwealth outposts. Britain, fearing isolation, moves into Europe. Will not New Zealand be left even more isolated?

AUSTRALIA

£127m. at stake. That is the economic aspect of Britain joining the Common Market as Australia sees it. Derived from the analysis prepared for the Cabinet's discussion with Mr. Sandys, it is the value of Australian exports, mainly farm produce, which are threatened with exclusion from both the United Kingdom and the European markets.

Superficially Australia's position resembles that of New Zealand in that she stands to lose an assured market for primary products dating from the last century, but a closer look discloses a happier position. Australia's biggest single export to the United Kingdom in 1960 was wool (£56½m.) which will be unaffected, except perhaps for the better. Second came meat (£38m.) covered by a 15-year agreement which ends in 1967. But an important difference here is that half of this meat was not the "difficult" or even unpopular lamb but beef. In the trade talks on prices for beef for 1964–7 which took place in Canberra in August, 1961, it emerged that Australian dependence on the British market had diminished and was likely to diminish still further when an obligation under which Australian beef producers have been required to offer all beef of first or second grade to Britain lapsed in October, 1961. Now Australia will be free to offer these better grades to America whose purchases exceeded Britain's in 1961 by about 70 per cent and at much better prices.

The third staple is dairy produce, £25m. in 1960, mainly butter £18m. and cheese £3½m. These will be hard hit. Fourth equal were cereals, almost exclusively wheat, and fruit (half tinned and half fresh or dried) to the value of roughly £20m. each. As regards wheat Sir John Teasdale, chairman of the Australian Wheat Board, considers the impact on Australian trade may not be as severe as was at first thought. In his view West European countries have been using subsidies, deficiency payments and other devices in an attempt to increase wheat production for years past and were not likely to obtain heavy increases, and in any case increase in land laid down to wheat would entail a corresponding decrease in land available for barley, oats, rye and other cereals. This may, however, be optimistic. France has wheat surpluses which she has openly announced she will hope to unload on the United Kingdom.

In return for these primary products, Britain exports to Australia a large miscellany of manufactured goods, chiefly chemicals £25m., iron and steel £13½m., metal £11m., machinery £81m., cars and commercial vehicles £43½m. But in recent years the value of these exports has been declining as a proportion of all manufactured goods imported. Britain's share has fallen from 70 per cent in 1954 to under 50 per cent in 1960. The gap has been filled largely by American overseas investments (e.g., Holden, General Motors Australian subsidiary) which are always well and profitably planned, and by a spectacular increase of Japanese sales to Australia following the signing of the Australian-Japanese trade agreement of July, 1957. Australia's home industries are producing more, too.

On balance, Australia might make up on the roundabouts what she lost on the swings, i.e. the expansion in her exports to a united Europe of wool, metals and meat (beef) might more than compensate for a decline in revenue from dairy produce (and perhaps wheat and fruit also).

It took nine hours for the Australians, under Mr. Menzies, to agree on the wording of the communiqué issued on Mr. Sandys' departure. Mr. Menzies, lawyer-politician, is, of course, one of the best-known and most respected Prime Ministers of the Commonwealth. The communiqué was chiefly remarkable for the special emphasis it laid on the political implications of Britain joining the Common Market. While recognising that "a powerful experienced group of free European nations can do much to preserve the world's peace", the fear was expressed that this might lead to a loosening of Commonwealth ties. With a population of only 10 million, Australia cannot forget the threat from her land-hungry and over-populated neighbours. Her chief military commitment is with ANZUS and she must look mainly to America for military defence, yet psychologically at least she would feel much safer in the arms of a strong Commonwealth, and despite assurances that the Commonwealth will be strengthened by the European venture, she fears that this will not, in fact, be so.

Meanwhile, a trade mission from Hong Kong has discussed in Canberra proposals for establishing a South-East Asia Common Market. The idea is supported by Tasmania who would like to see the United States playing a part in a "Pacific common trading bloc", but opposed by Malaya (partly because of Australia's immigration policy and partly because she is well-pleased with the deal her main exports, tin and rubber, will get in the Common Market) and of little interest to Japan who would prefer association with "the advanced western nations". It seems unlikely that any such regional arrangement would be regarded by Australia as a viable alternative to some sort of association with the Common Market.

CANADA

Canada has had the best of both worlds, the old and the new. She does not rely so heavily as Australia and New Zealand on her trade with the United Kingdom; in 1960 only 17 per cent of her exports were to Great Britain; trade with the United States which takes over half Canada's exports and supplies two-thirds of her imports was more than three times as great. But here is the rub—Canada's largest trade profit is with the United Kingdom. She cannot obtain such favourable terms from the economic giant to the South. She enjoys a favourable trade balance of over £100m. annually with the United Kingdom.

There have been some see-saws in Canada's exports to Britain, notably in iron and steel products which soared from £1m. in 1959 to £13m. in 1960 (now falling away): but the staples are three, cereals, metals and wood which together make up 75 per cent of her exports to Britain.

Firstly cereals, mostly wheat of the "hard" variety—exports to Britain for 1960 were worth £82m. It is known that restrictions covering agricultural imports to the EEC will be severe but, on the other hand, this particular Canadian wheat is irreplaceable by virtue of its unique quality.

Secondly and equally important are non-ferrous metals, exports of which to Britain rose steeply to £91m. in 1960. The position here has not been worked out in detail; copper and nickel would bear no duty, aluminium would face a ten per cent duty.

The third major export is wood in all its forms (timber £30m., pulp £12m., paper £30m.), and an appreciable amount of wooden furniture. Again the position is complex; soft wood lumber would enjoy duty-free entry but would lose its preference over non-Commonwealth suppliers, wood-pulp and newsprint would face a duty of between 5 and 8 per cent but, under the EFTA convention, the tariffs against Canada's chief competitors in wood-pulp, paper and paper-products were being reduced in any case.

In return Britain has found in Canada her best single export market for cars. Although exports to Canada had fallen in the first four months of 1961 to 16,000 (compared with 40,000 for the same period in 1960), this compares to a falling-off in sales of British cars to the United States from 72,000 to a mere 4,000 over the same period. Other big exports from Britain included machinery £53m. and chemicals £9m.

The overall picture, however, is of a great imbalance of trade; roughly Britain spends five dollars on Canadian goods for every three dollars spent by Canada on British goods. Canada is at best a difficult market for Britain, first the Atlantic to be bridged and then 18 million potential customers spread out in a 3,000 mile band in contrast to the short North to South communications which is all the United States, her chief competitor, has to contend with. Small wonder then if British businessmen resent the added handicap of having to face a continued erosion in the preferences accorded to British goods. Although since 1947 Canada has had the right under a bi-lateral agreement to modify or eliminate preferences, British exporters feel that there should be some "give and take" by Canada, not all take, for while Canada has been making things more difficult for British manufactures, Britain has been removing the last restrictions on the import of Canadian produce. Particularly resented by the British are the proposed changes in the rules on whether goods are "of a class or kind made in Canada"; the proposals of the Royal Commission (Canada) on the motor-car industry (although the $7\frac{1}{2}$ per cent excise tax which applied to all cars was removed in June, 1961, giving a welcome boost to the market, a 10 per cent import duty on cars was at one time under active consideration by the Canadian Government), and new rules governing subsidies to Canadian shipbuilding and shipping. High-flown phrases about "the historic right of Commonwealth free access to the British market" are apt to fall on deaf United Kingdom ears!

Politically the impact of Britain joining the Common Market would probably be greater on Canada than on any other nation of the Commonwealth. It will make it more difficult than ever for her to resist the strong pull from America. Will she become totally de-Europeanised? Mr. Diefenbaker and his Conservative Administration have always worked to preserve Canadian independence from America; Commonwealth and protectionist leanings have been a strong plank in their election platforms. Again, Canada wants the best of both worlds, to use Britain as a bulwark against Americanisation and yet to restrict trade with her. On the other hand, the leader of the Liberal opposition, Mr. Lester Pearson, though an advocate of free trade (he said of the Common Market "we should be jumping into this with both feet"), is no special friend of Britain. He was loud if not over-loud against her at the time of Suez and as Canada's representative to United Nations he has spent much time in the United States and is very well-disposed towards her.

Whichever party wins the next election, Britain's position will need careful handling. Fortunately the appointment of Lord Amory (the former Chancellor of the Exchequer) as U.K. High Commissioner in Ottawa could contribute much to clarifying the issues, and improving public relations between the two countries, always a sore point.

INDIA

India's Third Five-Year Plan, just announced, is in danger of being stillborn. Any setback in her export trade might necessitate the complete re-writing of this 774-page volume presented to the New Delhi Parliament on August 7, 1961. It seeks to provide for a population of 438 million people which is expected to rise to 492 million by 1966 and to 625 million by 1976. Its targets are to create 14 million new jobs and to provide 2,300 calories of food per day and 17·2 yards of cloth per annum for every citizen. This entails building a solid industrial base, keystone of which is a 163 per cent increase in steel production, raising it to 9·2m. tons per annum, supported by a 70 per cent increase in petroleum products and a 32 per cent increase in food, all to be achieved at the end of five years.

This ambitious blueprint might have to be torn up if India's export trade is undermined by Britain joining the Common Market. The two exports most affected would be tea and textiles. In 1960 Britain imported tea from India worth £56m., representing 62 per cent of the country's total shipments overseas, and £12·4m.

worth of textiles, about 33 per cent of India's total exports. Tea would bear an 18 per cent duty. Cotton textiles would face a duty unspecified at the moment, possible quota restrictions and severe competition.

India is worried about the status that Hong Kong (a colonial territory and also a competitor in textiles) and British East Africa (still at present a colonial territory and a competitor in tea) might be given; she hopes that they will not be given preferential treatment (as in the case of the French colonies at present). She would like negotiations with the Common Market to be in terms of commodities rather than of territories.

Other significant exports are hides and skins, unmanufactured tobacco (members of H.M. Forces will remember the "Victory" cigarettes issued to MEF in the last war!), oilseeds and oil cakes and jute manufactures. Except for tobacco (duty not yet fixed), they all enter the Common Market free.

The trade gap between the United Kingdom and India is negligible but there is an unfavourable gap with Common Market countries of some £105m. (India has been importing very considerably from West Germany). India had been hopeful of exporting light engineering goods, even sewing machines, to the United Kingdom, but that hope will almost certainly be dashed. Common Market countries are well ahead in the race both on grounds of quantity and quality, besides which protectionist devices would prohibit or restrict to a nonsensical quota the number of, e.g., sewing machines (under a recent quota decision, 34 Indian sewing machines were allowed into Italy!).

The Third Five-Year Plan was based on the assumption that India would not only maintain her present volume of exports, £487m. in 1960 but increase it to £562m. by the end of the five years. The present uncertainties, end how they may, must upset the planners, "the best-laid schemes of mice and men. . .", yet, in the long run, every move towards overall planning is likely to benefit India and to help her solve her vast problems. Has not Mr. Thorneycroft described the Common Market as "an outward-looking club anxious to expand world trade"? Moreover as Europe prospers, so European investment in India will tend to increase.

The phlegmatic Harrow-and-Cambridge educated Mr. Nehru, faced with stupendous difficulties, is reported to have been the least flurried and most business-like of all the Commonwealth heads encountered by Britain's three major missionaries, Mr. Sandys (Australia, New Zealand and Canada), Mr. Thorneycroft (India, Pakistan, Malaya, Singapore and Ceylon) and Mr. John Hare (West Africa and Rhodesia).

PAKISTAN

President Ayub Khan is basically sympathetic to the Common Market—"it would do a lot of good." He said at a Press Conference at Rawalpindi on October 3, 1961, that he hoped it would "lead to economic order in the non-Communist world". Pakistan's exports to the United Kingdom run at only about 19 per cent of her whole overseas trade. Her principal exports, raw cotton and jute, enter Europe duty-free already and would continue to do so; her greatest worry is that her manufactured goods, cotton textiles, surgical instruments, sports goods and jute manufactures do not compete in quality with those of Common Market countries.

In wishing to be associated with the Common Market, Pakistan would be pinning her hopes on the economic aid aspect rather than on any special advantages for her goods. She is not satisfied with her share of the economic aid handed out by the United States and Britain to date and would hope to receive, e.g., from the Overseas Development Fund of the Common Market, sums which she needs for her industrial expansion (a Russian team is at present prospecting, with high hopes, for oil there and capital will be needed to exploit this as well as other projects).

CEYLON

Ceylon's greatest worry is in regard to tea which instead of entering Britain (easily her biggest market) duty-free would bear an 18 per cent duty. It has been reckoned in Colombo that all in all, Ceylon tea might increase by as much as 10*d*. a pound. The resultant higher price would minimise the popularity of tea and expose Ceylon tea to competition from China and British East Africa.

MALAYA

Malaya has nothing to fear from the Common Market. Her preponderant export, rubber, would remain duty-free. Some fears about synthetic rubber, produced in Common Market countries, constituting a menace have been allayed. Tin, her other big export, would also enter duty-free.

GHANA

President Nkrumah of Ghana has one use for the Common Market—to make political capital out of it. For him it is a heaven-sent opportunity to denounce the European countries, especially Great Britain, and to set himself up as the champion of a free, united, politically and economically strong Africa. The Ghana News Agency reported his reaction:—"Nobody is against the European countries coming together but why do they want to draw us into their association? With my little knowledge of world economic problems, it is because they want to enslave us economically. They want to make us hewers of wood and drawers of water . . ."

This tiny state (population 6·7m.), only major export cocoa, has warned the sterling area that Ghana may be forced to leave it if Britain joins the Common Market!

Nkrumah, however, is a force to be reckoned with.

Eurafrica, the association of Common Market and French-speaking African states, held a successful conference in Strasbourg in the summer of 1961 and it is obvious that French-speaking African countries do derive great economic advantages from their present position, yet Nkrumah has just succeeded in negotiating a Customs Union with Upper Volta, which already belongs to the French West Africa Customs Union, and is giving it a loan in respect of loss of revenue from import duties which will increase its dependence on Ghana and increase the probability that it will be brought into the political union of Ghana, Guinea and Mali which Nkrumah has just set up. Nkrumah's activities are viewed with suspicion in Paris—he is trying now to seduce the tiny state of Dahomey (another French-speaking member of the West Africa Customs Union) into his orbit.

As his political opponents have discovered to their cost, one does not argue with the Communistic, opportunist Dr. Nkrumah. He is dynamic and aggressive and his stock stands high at the moment; he may, however, have overlooked the fact that rival producers of tropical beverages in Latin-America, with United States backing, might supply Common Market countries with cocoa (and coffee) if African supplies are too difficult.

NIGERIA

Nigeria is a rapidly developing country, and while her industries are growing she depends substantially on the receipts from her export crops.

Her principal export is cocoa (£35·1m. annually). She would like to increase her exports of cocoa to Common Market countries, in particular to West Germany and the Netherlands, but Britain takes a quarter of the total crop in respect of which Nigeria enjoys a preference she would like to retain.

Her second most important crop is ground-nuts

(£22m. annually). Here again, these enter Britain free of the 10 per cent duty payable by non-Commonwealth countries, as do her ground-nut oil, palm-oil and palm-kernel, thus putting her in a favourable position *vis-à-vis* her rivals.

If these exports can be safeguarded, Nigeria will certainly be helped rather than hindered by association with the Common Market. As a developing country she should qualify for technical assistance and aid. Over and above such help as she might be entitled to under the Common Market schemes, loans and economic aid from other sources would be more readily forthcoming if she were in a well-regulated association with Europe. However desirable an African Common Market may appear to certain sections of public opinion in Nigeria, it is clear that it is not feasible until the other African countries have achieved a broad-based economy of their own. Cocoa and ground-nuts are not enough. Nigeria, with a population of 34 millions (the largest population of any single British territory in Africa), is in a strong position where Common Markets are concerned.

RHODESIA

Though concerned with what will become of her important tobacco trade with Britain, Rhodesia is still more alarmed at the political implications of Britain joining the Common Market. She fears that it will mean the "final write-off of the Commonwealth" and make things even more difficult for the white man to keep his feet while the celebrated "winds of change" howl round him at hurricane force.

EIRE

The Irish Republic still enjoys Commonwealth preferences as if she were in fact a member of the Commonwealth. If Britain joined the Common Market without making some special arrangements to protect the free entry of Irish dairy products and meat to Britain, they would have to surmount the external tariff of the Common Market before entering the United Kingdom which the same products from Common Market countries would be entering free of charge.

Eire, therefore, decided to apply for full membership of the Common Market. At first "association" was thought to be the solution but this would have had the disadvantages that Eire would have had no voice in the formulation of policy and the danger that Irish produce might be denied full and free access to the Common Market and excluded from the benefits of the various Community Funds. In particular the European Fund for Structural Improvements in Agriculture should help Ireland, and during the difficult process of adapting Irish industry to free trade conditions she could draw too on the Social Fund which can provide half the cost of retraining and redeploying workers whose employment has been disturbed by the freeing of trade.

Doubts about the wisdom of allowing Europe's "major under-developed country" to join as a full member were largely dissolved by the charm, good sense and positive enthusiasm of the permanent Heads of the Eireann Departments of External Affairs and of Finance who toured the capitals of the Six.

Irish industry might then face full free trade by January, 1967, but it is understood that Mr. Sean Lemass hopes to secure some postponement of this date for the more sensitive industries. A pilot survey of the wool industry has been completed and working parties are producing reports on other industries. Few Irish industrialists are enthusiastic about entry into the Common Market where they would compete with highly organised and highly experienced manufacturers, but the problem may largely be one of reorientation and salesmanship.

The tourist industry is Eire's unexploited gold mine. Galway Bay, Roaring Water Bay, Dunmanus Bay, Bantry Bay and the Kenmare River (another bay!) would be tourist-ridden if they were on the continent of Europe.

The new airport at Cork should make a vast difference to the opening up of some of the grandest scenery in Europe, excellent roads are there already and the climate of South-West Cork is more that of Cornwall (fuchsias, palms and wild freesias—montbretia—line the roads and hedge the gardens) than of the Six Counties.

.   .   .

Enough has been said to show that there is not one Commonwealth problem but as many problems as there are Commonwealth countries—and more!

Africa should derive nothing but good from association with the Common Market. At the moment the French-speaking nations of Africa enjoy duty-free entry to the Common Market, the others do not. The arrangements under which these ex-French colonies are so generously treated come up for review in 1962 and it is hoped to extend generous terms to all producers of tropical produce—the ideal to be pursued is the gradual elimination of all tariffs on tropical produce.

Asian countries, India, Pakistan and Hong Kong pose the problem of low-cost and often low-quality manufactures. It is unlikely that the United Kingdom can absorb these, even for a transitional period, and the burden may be shared out generally among Common Market countries on a quota basis.

Besides regional difficulties, there are commodity difficulties. What of tea, bacon and New Zealand lamb? These peculiarities of the British diet are not sought after on the Continent and might be allowed free entry under the classification of "specialities".

Speculation on particular points is idle at the moment. Only detailed examination of all the facts and figures studied in the light of relevant world commodity positions and of the economic positions of the countries most involved will indicate possible solutions. Some countries may benefit temporarily from generous treatment meted out to a commodity which is of vital importance to a developing country—and others may be disappointed. It will be a grand shake-up, and give and take will be especially necessary in respect of butter, cheese, wheat, beef and fruit of which both Common Market countries and Commonwealth countries are large producers. In all temporary difficulties, the various Funds of the Community (suitably strengthened) will act as a buffer and in all long-term projects they may, bit by bit, take the place of "investment" by individual countries.

The thousand and one problems cannot be solved overnight. The first step will be to negotiate an elastic framework in which each Commonwealth country and each commodity can find a not impossible niche, the second to keep the position under constant review and revision.

But what of the political aspect, those much-talked of ties which have bound the countries of the Commonwealth together in a community of interest—and they have done that, intangible as they are. Useless to protest that they will continue as before. They cannot. This is a momentous change. But there is no reason to suppose that they will be replaced by ties more tenuous or less friendly. Quite the reverse. Everything indicates that with the Commonwealth moving into Europe (and Europe into the Commonwealth) an even better understanding will be the outcome. The age-old culture of Europe will be there for the Commonwealth countries to savour instead of merely Britain's questionable projection of herself by the Central Office of Information and the British Council—her "way of life".

But Great Britain will still be the "old country". The ties between Great Britain and the Commonwealth, less formal and more real, will become less those of the parent to the child and more those of an elder brother to a younger one, or of friend to friend.

INDUSTRY

When the Government came to consider industry, the question it had to ask itself was not whether Britain should join, but whether she could afford to stay out. In other words, could she afford to be on the wrong side of a tariff wall behind which 170 million people traded between themselves with the tremendous advantages that go with complete free trade, and who, by 1970 at the latest, would face the outside world as a solid trading bloc? British industry would thus face a two-pronged attack: it would be kept at arm's length in Europe owing to the tariff wall, and it would have to face the combined strength of the Six in all the other markets of the world, including those of the Commonwealth where the preferences granted to it are being eroded for the reasons already mentioned.

For a country whose very livelihood depends on large-scale trading, the prospect was clearly terrifying. "Exports go up or Britain goes down" is no empty phrase. Two-fifths of the working population of these islands are engaged in manufacturing, and manufactures provide about two-fifths of the total home output of goods and services. Nearly a third of Britain's manufactured products are exported.

Indeed, it is precisely this reliance on industry and a high level of exports which enables 52 million people to maintain one of the highest standards of living in the world. It enables Britain to indulge the luxury of having only 4 per cent of her population engaged in agriculture which means that she has to import one-half of all her foodstuffs.

Suffice it that the level of exports decline by a fraction and the whole of the economy is out of joint. A few strikes here and there, a slackening of exports and the Government has a balance of payments crisis on its hands.

It is the permanent fragility of the economy which has haunted Chancellors of the Exchequer since the end of the Second World War. One economic crisis has followed another. The same remedies have been applied —a strong dose of disinflation, through credit squeezes and restrictions on demand—and the economy has recovered, only to relapse into the bad old ways when the effects of the medicine have worn off.

The balance of payments crisis in the spring of 1961, which forced Britain to borrow $1,500m. from the International Monetary Fund in order to stave off a run on sterling, must have been decisive. It reminded the Government once again of the need for long-term remedies for our economic ills. It certainly was not engineered to coincide with the fateful Common Market question, but there is no denying that it was a powerful contributory factor to Britain's deciding to apply for membership. The Bankers of Basle (the Western central Banks) who held large sterling balances and who agreed once again, in March, 1961, to make gold and dollars available to the United Kingdom to bolster up its reserves, could not be expected to keep on bailing out the British Treasury as a matter of course. Britain in the Common Market would be a better subject for corrective financial measures on a Community basis than she would be left out in the cold, struggling against falling exports and diminishing markets.

A continued high level of exports, not merely in assured and steady markets but in expanding markets was, and is, a prerequisite of a sound United Kingdom economy. If such a level cannot be maintained, Britain will slip still farther back in the ranks of world powers, with a diminishing standard of living, increased unemployment leading, possibly, to social discontent and social disorders. She would no longer be able to hold on to her position as leading member of the Commonwealth and no longer be able to play her full part in NATO and the defence of the West. This prospect is not as fantastic as it sounds. History shows that the days of power and glory can be very short-lived.

No need, therefore, to doubt the necessity of sustaining the export drive. And to sustain it, no market could be ignored, least of all a market of 170 million on Britain's doorstep. It is true that United Kingdom exports to the Six have risen steadily, even after the signing of the Treaty of Rome. But this was because boom conditions applied everywhere and particularly in Europe.

It is also true that only 14 per cent of the United Kingdom's exports go to the Six whereas just over 40 per cent go to the Commonwealth. But whereas, as we have seen, the Commonwealth market shows all the signs of being a dwindling one, that of the Continent shows all the signs of being an expanding one and a rapidly expanding one at that. Furthermore, Britain's share of expanding world trade is diminishing. In 1950-60 the value of world exports of manufactures rose by 20 per cent. The value of United Kingdom exports only went up by 12 per cent, substantially less than was the case with the EEC countries, the USA and Japan. But this is not all. Even the United Kingdom's share of overseas sterling area trade is not keeping pace with that of other countries. The world's share increased by 19 per cent. The United Kindom's increase was only 9 per cent.

The rate of economic growth by the Six is superior to that of the United Kingdom. The GNP (Gross National Product) of the EEC countries is expected to rise by at least 5 per cent per annum whereas for the United Kingdom a 2 per cent growth is considered very reasonable. Intra-European trade is increasing more rapidly than that of any other area in the world.

Concentration and streamlining are making Continental industries more efficient, particularly in Germany. Productivity is among the highest in the world. Capital investment is on a higher scale than it is in the United Kingdom, and better use is often made of the capital invested.

This is not all due to the Common Market. Continental industry was well on the road, first to recovery, then to prosperity, before the Treaty of Rome was negotiated. But the Common Market has made certain that the impetus was maintained where it might have flagged!

Its task now is to see that Europe moves forward as a compact bloc of nations ready to meet all political and economic challenges from whatever source.

Joining the Common Market will mean the end of a 30-year period of high protectionism which started in Ottawa in 1932. British industry will receive a salutary jolt; it will have to take its place alongside the giant industrial complexes of Germany and the lesser giants of France and Italy, in many cases now linked with the Germans. This is the greatest challenge industry in the United Kingdom has ever had to face. It should now be girding itself for a battle with the scientist, the technologist and the salesman at a high premium.

The changes which will be brought about by joining the Common Market can be summarised as follows:

1. The markets of the Six will be thrown open to British industry and vice versa.

2. The preferences United Kingdom exports enjoy in Commonwealth countries will disappear because the United Kingdom Government will be required to follow the import-export policies of the Six. The only

way the United Kingdom could continue to enjoy Imperial preferences would be for these preferences to be given without reciprocity or for them to be extended to the Six. No Commonwealth country has any intention of doing either unless, at a later stage, mutually satisfactory commercial agreements can be negotiated with the Six. This is certainly a long-term possibility but it is not an immediate one. British exports to the Commonwealth amounted to over £1,400m. in 1960. About half of them enjoyed preferences varying from $7\frac{1}{2}$ per cent to 33 per cent. The range of goods over which the preferences spread was highest in the case of Australia and New Zealand (about 90 per cent) and Canada (80 per cent).

African territories like Kenya, Uganda, Tanganyika, Nigeria, Ghana give no preference at all to United Kingdom imports, although 75 per cent of their exports to the United Kingdom receive some form of preference.

India, Pakistan, Singapore and Hong Kong grant only very limited preferences.

3. The preferences granted by the United Kingdom to manufactured imports from Commonwealth countries will also disappear. These imports are not of great importance. In the case of Canada they concern mostly machinery and finished manufactures imported at times of boom when availability rather than price is the main attraction. They might have concerned India in the coming years since she had hoped to expand her exports of light-engineering products to Britain under the preferential tariff.

4. Industries which import raw materials from the Commonwealth will have to do so under the common external tariff of the Six. Many of these materials will enter Britain and the Common Market countries free of duty, e.g., tin, flax, rubber, hemp, sisal, jute, wool, copper, nickel, etc. Others such as aluminium, lead and

zinc bars, wood and wood-pulp, newsprint, will pay a duty not exceeding 10 per cent. Paper (other than newsprint) will pay 14–21 per cent.

These profound changes in the United Kingdom tariff system which will inevitably put up the price of many imported raw materials and semi-manufactured goods, will bring about corresponding changes in the structure and methods of British industry. Large firms with powerful financial resources will fare better than small firms because reorganisation will be easier—or less painful. The less efficient businesses, and efficiency will be the acid test of survival, may well be absorbed by bigger firms.

Where the lack of efficiency has come from faulty management the workers will be absorbed by the bigger firms. Where it has come from lack of skill or craftsmanship from the workers, those put out of work may find employment in other trades. Their case is provided for under the Treaty by the European Social Fund whose task it is to see that rationalisation does not cause permanent unemployment.

On the contrary, the purpose of the Community and Britain's membership of it is to keep employment at a high level, by overall planning.

Firms—and there are large numbers—which have not up to now paid much attention to exports, will have to do so or see their businesses dwindle. Survival in some cases may come through specialisation. In others it may come through tie-ups with Continental firms. It should be remembered that under the Common Market the movement of capital and labour will eventually be free. This will facilitate the interlocking of British and Continental industry and some important link-ups are foreseen, particularly between the large combines in steel, chemicals, electrical and mechanical engineering, motor-car and aircraft construction. Some important tie-ups exist already. The tendency will be for them to be reinforced. But the keynote to success will undoubtedly be in the first instance the ability to keep costs down and prices competitive. Keeping costs down means relating them to wages and productivity which means that go-slow movements, wild-cat strikes, frivolous stoppages and futile arguments about who drills through what first will be a luxury no one can afford. More than ever management and unions will have to keep labour disputes down to a minimum.

In 1957 the Economist Intelligence Unit produced a long and brilliant analysis of the impact of a Free Trade Area on British industry. The Free Trade Area never came into being, but most of what the EIU said at the time holds good today. It issued the significant warning, which the Government took to heart, that the majority of British industries would suffer if a Common Market only came into being. The Government faced this prospect in the spring of 1961 and reacted to it by deciding to apply for membership.

The EIU put the whole of the British manufacturing industry into five groups and classified each industry according to how it would fare in a Free Trade Area. Although conditions will not be so favourable in a Common Market as they would have been in a Free Trade Area, particularly in the case of industries importing certain raw materials from the Commonwealth such as aluminium, lead and zinc which will pay a duty of up to 10 per cent, the analysis still gives an excellent guide to the probable performances in each sector of industry. (Percentages given are approximate.)

Group I   INDUSTRIES GAINING: Motor vehicles, chemicals, wool, electrical engineering, general engineering, rubber manufactures, iron and steel, hosiery and clothing. (These industries produce nearly 60 per cent of the total output of manufactures and employ nearly 60 per cent of the manpower.)

Group II INDUSTRIES PROBABLY GAINING: Non-ferrous metals, metal manufactures, aircraft, ship-building and marine engineering, oil refining, building materials, glass, scientific instruments, sports goods. (22 per cent of total output, 24 per cent of total manpower.)

Group III INDUSTRIES LOSING: Cotton, man-made fibres, paper, leather, watches and clocks. (11·8 per cent of total output, 9·7 per cent of total manpower.)

Group IV INDUSTRIES PROBABLY LOSING: China, foot-wear, toys. (2·9 per cent of total output, 3·1 per cent of total manpower.)

Group V INDUSTRIES LEAST AFFECTED: Railway vehicles, furniture, jute. (4·1 per cent of total output, 4·9 per cent of total manpower.)

From these figures it will be seen that 60 per cent of industry stands to gain in any case and 22 per cent are probable gainers. The scales will be tipped in their favour if trading conditions turn out to be more favourable than at first supposed and provided maximum efficiency is attained.

Some practices will have to go, such as the dual pricing of coal and artificial restraints in the steel industry. The latter include the fixing of maximum prices at home and the control of scrap sales. The steel industry may have to charge more to the domestic consumer but because of transport charges which would apply to the sale of continental steel in Britain, the price of United Kingdom steel would still compare favourably with that of the Six. The huge investment plans and increased costs of the UK steel industry had the effect in any case of raising the maximum home price of steel in the summer of 1961.

In the non-ferrous metal industries, increased trade may be limited owing to the tendency more and more to refine on the spot abroad. Germany and France are the United Kingdom's greatest competitors here.

In the metal manufacturing industries, special or quality items should do well such as press tools, high quality cutlery, locks, safes. Metal window-frame shapes may have to be altered to suit continental tastes and that goes for many other articles, such as motor-cars, where British conservatism is not necessarily a virtue, particularly when craftsmanship and finish is below standard. The radio and TV industry will have to switch en bloc to the 625-line screen. Post-sales service will play an important part in increased sales.

The United Kingdom has a particularly good record and leads the way in electronically-controlled machine tools but in ordinary machine tools Germany is firmly established on the Continent and will be the United Kingdom's most formidable competitor.

Indeed, in industry, the Germans, French and Italians combined provide a staggering challenge to their British rivals. Between them they cover the whole field of general, electrical and mechanical engineering. British scientists and technicians will have their work cut out to match and surpass the ever-improving skills and techniques of their opposite numbers on the Continent. But it is the sort of challenge to which British industrialists and scientists have always responded whole-heartedly as British invention during two world wars has shown.

But why the challenge at all? Why choose deliberately to plunge head-first into a market where competition is at its most severe? Why not concentrate on developing the Commonwealth? These questions are often asked. The answer most industrialists and the Government have given is that Britain must keep in the race with the giants on her doorstep. If she does not, she will not in any case be in a position to hold on to her rôle in the Commonwealth and her status in the world at large, leave alone expand it.

As far as the United Kingdom consumer of manufactured goods is concerned, the net effect of continental competition should be to give him a wider choice and bring prices down on many articles such as cars, radio and TV sets, washing-machines, refrigerators, etc. One inestimable blessing: purchase-tax, that ugly Second World War fungus, may have to go completely!

AGRICULTURE

It is essential to get agriculture into a proper perspective because it is very well-organised, extremely vocal if not vociferous, and the propaganda given to its "plight" under the Common Market has had certain political overtones. The Conservative Party is not only supported by the majority of rural constituencies (to be weighed against Labour's lion's share of purely industrial constituences), but in the marginal seats, clustered on the edge of big cities, are to be found a great number of growers of tomatoes and early vegetables.

Agriculture, in a sense, is no more than just another of Britain's many industries. It occupies only 4 per cent of the working population, i.e. 1,000,000 people out of a working population of 24,800,000. General engineering (i.e. excluding electrical and shipbuilding engineering) alone employs nearly a million workers.

Government agricultural policy is founded on the Agriculture Acts of 1947 and 1957. In February each year the Ministry of Agriculture in consultation with the farmers' unions determines guaranteed prices for fat cattle, sheep, pigs, eggs, wool, milk, cereals, potatoes and sugar-beet. If, in fact, prices realised for livestock, livestock products and crops are less than the guaranteed prices, then the difference is made good by a Government "deficiency payment", usually to the appropriate Marketing Board (Milk, Potato, British Wool, etc.) which distributes it. Detailed arrangements naturally vary for different commodities.

Over and above this, various grants-in-aid of particular

kinds of production or farming practice known as production grants are payable. Grants are made for fertilisers and limes (more than half the cost of liming land is refundable), ploughing up land that has been down to grass for not less than three years, for constructing and improving silos (about half the cost), etc. In addition grants for long-term improvements are available; towards the cost of improving farm buildings, roads and fences and the supply of electricity (approximately one-third of the cost), towards land drainage (up to one-half), and towards water supply. The total cost of all this agricultural support (by subsidies at the expense of the taxpayer) rose from £241·4m. in 1958-9 to £259·1m. for 1959-60. Although costly it is a successful system. Since its inception very large increases have taken place in all the main products except oats and potatoes. Before the war Britain produced (in terms of value) about one-third of its food, it now produces about one-half. British agriculture rests comfortably on a great industrial base which supports it in the style to which it has been accustomed since the last war. But this system is not at all suited to the Six because they do not have an economic base large enough to support their much larger and much poorer agricultural population (20 per cent average for all Common Market countries as against Britain's 4-5 per cent).

The EEC in search of a single price level throughout the Common Market at present proposes three categories. The first concerns only cereals, milk and milk products (butter, cheese, etc.) and sugar-beet (in all 35 per cent of British agricultural output). For each product a target price will be fixed annually. These target prices differ from the British guaranteed prices in two important ways. First they are wholesale prices not prices at the farm, and second the European Cereals Bureau, the Sugar Bureau and the Milk Bureau will intervene in the market (by buying) only if the price falls by a certain margin below the target (5–7 per cent approx.).

The second category comprises meat and eggs. There will be no target price system for these products but protection will be by common tariff (20 per cent for beef). A minimum import price and an import levy may be used additionally, and a Bureau set up to deal with these products may intervene in the market with monies derived from levies.

For fruit, vegetables and wine, there will be no Bureau. Protection will be by common external tariff and if necessary, control of imports by a quota system.

The prospect for British agriculture hinges mainly on whether the level of prices established by the EEC would be higher than the present British guaranteed prices or not. The following table gives a reasonably reliable forecast.

Comparison of average EEC price and of UK guaranteed price (with deficiency payment) expressed as a percentage

	EEC	UK
Wheat	124	100
Barley	104	100
Beef	113	100
Lamb	100-plus (quality higher in C.M., less mutton, prices much higher)	100
Milk	100	122
Eggs	100	106·5
Sugar	100	111
Fruit and vegetables	100	100-plus (UK prices mostly much higher)

From this it will be seen that wheat, barley, beef and lamb should fare much better in the Common Market as the price-level should be higher than that at present obtaining in the United Kingdom. Dairy farming might do worse, but it must be remembered that milk is essentially a local product and not easily brought into a Common Market system. Eggs, sugar-beet and horticulture might be expected to do worse. (British horticulture at present enjoys protection not through guaranteed prices, as is the case with agriculture, but through import duties which on some produce such as tomatoes reach 150 per cent at certain times of the year. Imports are only allowed to enter freely at times when they do not compete with the home crops. In the long run very keen competition would be expected from Holland's low-cost high-quality horticulture, already organised for export, and from Italy. Here again, the perishable nature of much produce makes home distribution advisable.)

British agriculture is in good heart thanks to the improvements which have been freely available under the present system; the fertiliser and lime subsidy for 1959–60 was £40m., the tractor density is one of the greatest in the world, one to every 34 acres of arable land. Only the mental adjustment is lacking. NFU spokesmen are still canvassing for deficiency payments and the *status quo*. There can be no *status quo*. Britain has come to the crossroads. She could, in any case, no longer afford to go on paying huge subsidies to agriculture each year from the diminishing receipts from her manufacturing industry. Allegations of "feather-bedding" are not altogether short of the mark. British agriculture has had no worries comparable to those of other industries which have had to struggle with the cold world outside these islands for their living. Export markets can be very hard to find and to hold—while directors and executives of Britain's factories big and small, from ICI to the newest and bravest little plastics factory, have been facing up to the chill winds of competition (developing high blood pressure in the process) the farmer has walked, financially, in England's green and pleasant land. If British factories are prepared to take on West German factories in fair and equal combat, so should British farmers be prepared to take on the efficient agricultural producers of the Common Market—France and Holland (not Germany whose farming population of one-fifth is probably the least efficient of all).

Although it is unthinkable that because they are strong in the lobby, British farming interests should take it upon themselves to dictate to the Government as to whether or not Britain should join the Common Market, basing their objections purely on sectional interests, considerable sympathy must be felt with a section of the community which has put its house in order only to find that that particular order must be changed in favour of another and as yet largely unspecified order. The uncertainty is the aspect which farmers most dislike. At the moment farmers' incomes are not determined by the price at which their products are sold in the market; under the Common Market, they would be.

There are also dark memories on the farms of the "Cinderella" days when whilst British industry was allowed to forge ahead selling its manufactured goods the world over, home agriculture was dismissed with a shrug of the shoulders—could not food come in from the New World and the Antipodes in exchange for manufactured goods? In 1930 the bottom of a long depression in British agriculture was reached and even by the outbreak of war in 1939 much had been proposed but too little done. The lean days of the U-boat blockade will not easily be forgotten.

Good public relations between the farmers and the Government are absolutely indispensable, either using the National Farmers' Union, heavily committed as they are against the Common Market, or some other suitable channel of information. But given up-to-date accurate bulletins on what is happening, there is no reason to suppose that the British farmer will not give a good account of himself at all stages. The changes will take place gradually and so far the emphasis in all discussion on the Mansholt proposals (outlined above, named after Dr. Mansholt, Dutch vice-president of the Commission, who is responsible for agriculture) has been on flexibility. Moreover the British farmer will be able to make his voice heard at every stage of the negotiations.

Horticulture must pin its hopes largely on the efficiency of the Horticultural Marketing Council, set up under the Horticultural Act, 1960, with the object of improving the marketing and distribution of and developing the trade in horticultural produce, collecting and distributing information about supply, demand and prices, encouraging better grading and carrying out research. Until it knows what it is likely to be up against, the horticultural industry cannot plan. The Council, to be financed from public funds during its first three years of operation and eventually by the horticultural industry, should already be studying the methods and marketing of the Dutch and Italian horticulturists and examining market possibilities.

And what of the consumer? Estimates of the effect on the retail price of food are so variable as to be largely guesses but vary from a rise of one-half per cent to three per cent in the cost-of-living index. An important point is that the Government would be saving perhaps as much as £180m. of the present subsidy to agriculture which could bring substantial relief to the taxpayer to offset any rise in the cost of living.

"Some sovereignty will have to be surrendered, and before making any final comment we should know how far this is to go and how far the British economy is to be subject to influences outside the Government and the House of Commons."— LORD CHANDOS, chairman of Associated Electrical Industries.

Chapter Seven

SOVEREIGNTY AND THE TREATY OF ROME

ALL treaties and agreements imply a diminution of sovereignty in the sense that those who sign them are bound, at least morally, to fulfil the obligations they have contracted therein. They are, therefore, that much less free than they were before they signed.

The loss of sovereignty that goes with the Treaty of Rome, however, is of a different order. The Six nations have delegated many of their powers to a Commission, which, under the Treaty, enjoys a considerable measure of independence and can take decisions and issue regulations which are binding on the signatory governments. Such a delegation of powers is exceptional. It does not exist in the case of any other treaty or agreement signed by Britain. It is what makes European integration work.

In the early stages of implementation, power is divided unequally. The ultimate power of decision on important issues is given to the Council of Ministers. But as time goes on the position is progressively reversed and the Commission takes over wide powers to run the Community unhampered by the veto.

The power of veto by any one nation is retained only during the first and second stages on many of the important subjects, such as agriculture, transport and commercial policy. During the third stage and thereafter, only a combination of powers can veto proposals by the Commission on these subjects. In the case of the approximation of laws, the veto only applies during the first stage. On the other hand where the Six are required to co-ordinate their long-term economic planning in the light of economic trends (*la politique de conjoncture*— Article 103) the veto applies permanently where the adoption of plans or measures is concerned. The implementation of these plans or measures by the Commission is not, however, subject to the veto.

The power of veto exists permanently also in the case of the admission or association of new members and alterations to the composition of the Commission.

It also exists where the Council must decide whether or not each of the three stages of 4 years has been carried out satisfactorily in accordance with the terms of the Treaty. But here the veto is not final. Where the passage from the first to the second stage is concerned—a decision on this point will have to be taken by the end of 1961—the effect of the veto is to prolong the first stage by one, or at most, two years. After that a qualified or weighted majority is sufficient to pass from stage one to stage two. If even a qualified majority is not forthcoming an Arbitration Board appointed by the Court of Justice decides the issue.

The duration of stages two and three cannot be curtailed except by a unanimous vote and cannot be extended if the effect of such extension is to prolong the total transitional stage beyond fifteen years, i.e. beyond 1972.

In some cases during the third and final stage, and certainly after the transitional period is over, the Council will take most of its decisions connected with the implementation of the Treaty either by a simple majority (on matters of minor importance) or by a qualified majority on a proposal of the Commission. The cases where the veto will still apply are strictly limited, as already mentioned. It does not apply, incidentally, to revision of the Treaty for which a special procedure is laid down under Article 236.

The qualified or weighted voting system is a complex one. Its purpose is to protect the Commission against the Council and the smaller Powers against the Big Three (France, Germany and Italy). For instance, when the Council is voting under this system on a proposal submitted by the Commission, any 12 votes are sufficient, which means that one of the Big Three acting singly cannot prevent the adoption of the proposal nor can the Benelux countries, acting as a bloc. On the other hand, when the Council is acting independently of the Commission but still under the qualified majority rule, the requisite 12 votes must include the votes of at least four Powers, which means that the Big Three cannot gang up against the Benelux countries.

Britain's entry into the Common Market will raise delicate issues of prestige on this question of majority voting. So will the entry of other EFTA countries such as Norway and Denmark. The present system with its carefully weighted checks and balances will be thrown completely out of gear. The search for a new voting formula which will preserve roughly the same equilibrium will be no easy task if national prides are not to be hurt.

The other adjustments needed to the Treaty do not, fortunately, raise the same problems. Britain will have one, or perhaps two, members (the maximum any one state is allowed to have is two) on the Commission and proper representation in the Assembly and on the various committees, the European Investment Bank, the Overseas Development Fund, the Social Fund, etc. But here again, it will be necessary to preserve the ratios as far as possible. Presumably a British judge or jurist will be appointed to the Court of Justice.

Effects of the Diminution of National Sovereignty

The Ministries most concerned during the transitional

stages with derogations of sovereignty will be the Treasury, the Board of Trade, the Ministry of Agriculture, the Ministry of Transport, the Home Office and the Attorney-General's Department, all of which are intimately connected with vital aspects of EEC policy. The Foreign Office will naturally have a permanent interest in the activities of the Community because of the overall effects of membership on foreign policy. In due course, however, almost all Ministries and Government Departments will be affected in one way or another and few institutions of the realm, even the most cherished, will escape the backwash.

The Board of Trade will have one of its major functions taken away: that of concluding commercial agreements with the outside world. This function will be taken over by the European Commission (Art. 228). It is one of the most significant changes brought about by Britain's entry because commercial agreements are so often closely linked with foreign policy as a bargaining weapon.

The Board of Trade will no longer be able independently to alter tariffs or quotas either with the Commonwealth or with the outside world except by permission of the Commission or the Council. It will have to co-ordinate its commercial policies with those of the Community as a whole (Articles 110–116).

Much the same applies to the Treasury. Budgetary and balance of payments problems will still be very much its concern, but here again close consultation and concerted action with the Community on financial policy generally will be required. It will have to maintain constant contact with the Monetary Committee of the Community which gives advice to both the Commission and the Council. The Treasury will have a specific obligation, under Articles 95–99, not to pursue fiscal policies which will in any way conflict with the common trading rules of the Community. This applies to levies, turnover taxes, excise duties and other forms of indirect taxation. It will also have a duty, under Article 103, to look upon long-term planning as a common interest. In the present state of Britain's balance of payments difficulties and persistent economic malaise this may be more of a blessing than a burden.

The harmonisation of domestic—or municipal—laws by the Six and subsequent members, poses a complex problem for the Attorney-General's Department and the Home Office owing to the different legal systems in force on the Continent and in Britain. Article 100 calls for the "approximation of such legislative and administrative provisions of the Member States as have a direct incidence on the establishment or functioning of the Common Market".

Community law will have a long arm of its own. Under Article 211, it shall "in each Member State possess the most extensive legal capacity accorded to legal persons under their respective municipal law". It may in particular "acquire or transfer movable and immovable property and may sue and be sued in its own name". It will certainly be a novelty in English law that regulations issued by foreign institutions such as the Commission and the Council shall automatically have force of law in England (Article 189) and that sanctions such as fines, imposed by these institutions (Article 192) on British citizens or bodies possessing legal personality, for violations of these regulations shall be enforceable in British courts whereas an appeal against such sanctions lies not to the latter but with the Court of Justice of the Community.

The Ministry of Agriculture, vitally affected by Articles 38–45, will have the unenviable task of adjusting its farm policy of guaranteed prices, subsidies and deficiency payments to whatever policy is finally agreed upon when Britain joins. Indeed, Ministers have hinted that the present system may have to be scrapped altogether and a new one adopted more in line with the

Common Market system of minimum prices, levies and import duties, once this system has been put into final shape.

The Ministry of Transport has a less onerous task. Its present plans for improving the road network of Britain may have to be altered to fit in with the ambitious schemes for vast and fast European highways now being worked out by the Commission's Transport Committee. Immediate improvements to the highways of South-East England may have to be started to deal with the possibility of vastly increased traffic if and when the Channel Tunnel (or bridge) scheme is finally approved. The links between the Ministry of Transport and the Community are likely to be an undisguised blessing as any constant user of the roads of England will agree. Roman law may not be to the liking of the British jurist, but Roman roads, built in the modern style, would be very much to the liking of the British motorist.

The Monarchy and Parliament are two of the most cherished institutions in the land. The first will not be affected. The Queen will still be Queen of the United Kingdom and Northern Ireland, Canada, Australia, New Zealand, etc., and Head of the Commonwealth. But Parliament may well find that in practice many of its powers and functions will be slowly eroded in favour of those of the Community's institutions—the Assembly, or Parliament, the Council of Ministers, the Commission and the Court of Justice. The Parliament in Britain is virtually all-powerful. It can alter or abolish any law in the land. But it will be unable to alter any of the laws of the Community. Some of these laws, as we have seen, will be directly enforceable in Britain. Others will be carried out by the Government. If it criticises the Government in certain fields of policy, it will in effect be criticising the Community and more often than not, the Commission. This could be done with greater effect in the Assembly of the Community where all parties at

Westminster will be represented. Its control over the activities of Ministers will virtually disappear on issues in which these Ministers are themselves no longer free agents, in the sense that they will be members of a team directed from Brussels, the HQ of the Commission, and carrying out a common policy.

It will be free to overthrow the Government on these issues—and they may be important, but the following Government will be bound by the same obligations towards the Community as was its predecessor. So little will be gained.

The sweeping party attack based on political doctrine and delivered with colourful oratory and not a few clichés, will become increasingly more irrelevant because the party in power will always be able to plead that in many fields of policy it is merely acting as a member of a team. Blame the Community, yes, but not the Government for carrying out the Community's policies! As political unity develops in Europe, even on foreign affairs the Government may well be able to shelter, if it wants to, behind the Community.

In the first announcements of its new policy, the Conservative Government played down the derogation of sovereignty aspect—presumably to sweeten the pill, but as the years go by M.P.s will find—to many it has occurred already—that whereas on paper they are endowed with vast legislative powers and powers of control over the Government, these powers amount to very little in practice.

Their field of action has already been narrowed in defence and economic affairs by Britain's membership of a multiplicity of international organisations including NATO and OEEC (now OECD). If many internal economic matters and to a large extent Commonwealth and foreign affairs are to come under the wing of the European Community, there will be very little room left for useful debate at Westminster.

An important point arises from the loosening of links with the Commonwealth: In the past, colonial territories acquiring independence remained within the Commonwealth and enjoyed what was left of Commonwealth preference with the United Kingdom. The jump will be from tutelage straight into the outside world whereas before, the Commonwealth Relations Office provided a convenient half-way shelter to complete independence. Now, once a colony is given independence it will move automatically out of the orbit of Westminster. Its links with the United Kingdom will be maintained via Brussels.

This erosion of the useful functions of Parliament will soon leave M.P.s with little else to do but to keep an eye on the purely domestic aspects of government and watch over the day-to-day interests of their constituents—tasks to which many M.P.s are well-suited.

This is not necessarily an argument against Britain's joining but it does bring grist to the mill of the anti-Common Marketeers who are opposed to British participation on other grounds.

It raises the question, also, of whether the Government should go to the country on an issue of this magnitude. There is no constitutional obligation on it to do so but it can be argued that the Government have a *moral* obligation to do so. To do the right thing is often the right thing to do! H. R. G. Greaves in his *British Constitution* asserts that it is now a convention of the constitution "that Governments do not impose legislation of a keenly controversial nature . . . and there is no denying that the Common Market issue is keenly controversial . . . unless they have a mandate from the electorate". Greaves is not gospel on the constitution, but the argument carries much weight. The Government could act on a mandate in two ways. It could consider that the mandate given to it in 1959 was sufficient, or it could seek a new mandate. The first course would require an impossible stretching of the imagination. The second would require an election which the Conservative Party might not feel at all sure of winning on other grounds although if the battle was fought on the single issue of the Common Market, it might scrape through.

As the Common Market question is far from clear-cut and cuts across all parties, except the Liberals, the chances of it forming the sole issue at an election would be small. In these circumstances the Government may agree with that other constitutional expert, Sir Ivor Jennings, and consider that it does not need a specific mandate to go in. In which case, by mustering its legions, and issuing a three-line whip at Westminster, it could no doubt get home with a comfortable majority. The division which took place at the end of the two-day debate in the House of Commons following the Prime Minister's announcement on July 31, 1961, must have been comforting. All the recalcitrants except one merely abstained from voting. True, the terms of admission to the EEC were not known but, as Lord Silkin argued in the House of Lords, the Government, after nine months of patient exploration with the Six and long talks with the Commonwealth Governments, are unlikely to have started negotiations without feeling reasonably certain that they would succeed and that the conditions of entry would not be too onerous.

A last argument against an election: the historical precedents are against it and that, for Mr. Macmillan, with his keen eye for historical parallels, should be conclusive. Peel's rescission of the Corn Laws split the Tory Party from top to bottom. It took them a generation to recover. Tariffs brought down the Conservative Governments of Balfour in 1905, and of Baldwin in 1923. Far better to go ahead with the present safe majority of 100! Even so, some constitutional lawyers and not a few members of the public would still consider that on the whole the Government had acted improperly.

Chapter Eight

WHAT THE PARTIES AND THE UNIONS THINK

Labour Party and the Trade Unions

The Labour Party and the Unions, like the Conservatives themselves, are keenly divided on this issue and in some cases for the same reasons.

In all three there is the fundamental belief, which no amount of facts, figures or logic will dislodge, that it will be a bad, bad day for England when she surrenders her sovereignty to the point where she has to take orders from a Commission sitting in Brussels, composed of a dozen or more foreign economists or lawyers, on how to run not only her own affairs but those of the Commonwealth as well. The Commonwealth is so essentially English that it should never be consciously broken up by the United Kingdom Government, of all governments. This belief is a powerful mixture of chauvinism, instinct, and in some cases sound common sense. It belongs to no class in particular. It runs like a thread through the fabric of British life. It brings all classes together in a common suspicion of the foreigner however pleasant or able he may be.

But over and above this somewhat emotional approach, there are many people in the Labour Party and the Unions who dislike the Common Market and the people who run it on grounds of political doctrine. Not only are the principles of the Common Market—free and fair competition based on free enterprise—the very opposite of what a good Socialist should cherish but the men at the top, the De Gaulles, the Adenauers and those around them, are undemocratic, reactionary and quite incapable of reaching reasonable agreement with the Russians on the future of Germany and Europe generally. Their power rests mainly on the Christian Democracy of the Centre parties most of which are Catholic and therefore automatically suspect in the eyes of the large Nonconformist element in the Labour movement. The long arm of the Vatican is seen behind all Catholic and Right-Wing movements in Europe and the Vatican must, by definition, be anti-Communist—which, of course, it is.

This opposition in principle to the men of Europe is summed up in its mildest form by Denis Healey, Labour's spokesman on foreign affairs, when he wrote: "It is not simply a question of whether we should be prepared to limit our sovereignty in general—I believe we should. It is whether the political attitudes of our prospective partners and the institutions they have set up in their Community make it desirable for us to limit our diplomatic freedom in this particular framework." (*Observer*, May 28, 1961.) Denis Healey is a Right-Wing member of the party. The same views were put more pungently by seven Labour M.P.s, all of whom lean in varying degrees to the Left. They were the Rt. Hon. Emanuel Shinwell, Sir Leslie Plummer, Mr. John Dugdale, Mr. Ellis Smith, Mr. Norman Pentland, Mr. Michael Foot and Mr. Anthony Greenwood.

In a letter to *The Times* they implied that those who recommended membership of the Common Market were defeatists who were "snatching at the speculative lifeboat of so-called European unity". These defeatists, who made light of the high quality of British skills and industrial techniques, were trying to induce the country "to accept not only economic but political integration with Italy, harassed by over-population and unemployment problems; a divided Germany, seething with bitterness and ideological differences; West Germany, preoccupied by thoughts of restoring lost territories; France, engaged in an internal revolt by its peasantry and external colonial troubles, with no bright record of political stability; and the Belgian coal industry almost in ruins."

There are many Conservatives, and perhaps some Liberals, who would secretly agree with all these views, but the common thread of patriotism is provided by the following comments of Mr. P. Lynch, Chairman of the 115,000-strong National Union of Tailors and Garment Workers: "It would be better to retain the historical kinship of the British Commonwealth than exchange even some part of the family heritage for the doubtful friendship of General de Gaulle and Dr. Adenauer."

On the economic side it is clear Labour does not like some aspects of the Common Market. Harold Wilson, the Party's spokesman on economic affairs, said of it in the House of Commons on August 3, 1961: "Let us be frank about it. This is a highly restrictive, discriminating, trading bloc. We should have no illusions about it."

The leader of the Party, Hugh Gaitskell, led for some time from the fence on this issue, sensing, rightly, that the disarray in the Conservative Party was as great as it was in the Labour Party.

As for the Trade Unions, they have constantly said that they are in favour of the greatest possible trade with the EEC, with EFTA and with the "Iron Curtain" countries, which commits them to strictly nothing. However, in the special report presented to the annual congress of the TUC at Portsmouth in 1961, Trade Union leaders expressed considerable doubt about the economic value of joining the Common Market and suggested that the policies of the Six should be modified in several ways in order to make it possible for Britain to join. The report was drawn up in close consultation with Labour Party leaders and it followed the party line laid down by Gaitskell, that before the party could decide it would have to know the terms of admission.

Basically, of course, like the political theorists of the party, many Left-Wing Trade Unionists fear that membership would prevent any future Labour government from re-introducing Socialism in Britain and carrying out further nationalisations. A favourite argument of the militant Left-Winger is: "We're not going to be bossed by the Brussels bureaucracy". "We're not going to be told what we can nationalise and what we can't." They fear a loss of power of the Unions in their relations with employers and management. They argue that EEC policy will favour the employers as against the workers because of its emphasis on efficiency. Employers will shelter behind the economic, social and labour rules of the Brussels club in an attempt to discipline the unions. They will argue that to meet EEC requirements, and more particularly to meet Continental competition, wages will have to be closely related to productivity otherwise British industry will price itself out of European and world markets. Full employment, however much inefficiency it entails, has been a watchword with Labour and the Trade Unions. Yet full employment, as every employer knows, does not always lead to efficiency and high production, both of which are essential to steady economic growth.

A national wages policy will be more of a necessity than ever. Automatic free-for-all wage demands will merely aggravate any economic crisis, as they have done for years. "More pay for less work" is a motto which will have no impact on managements struggling to keep their businesses above water or fighting to retain important home and foreign markets.

It should be remembered that just as we shall try to sell more on the Continent so the Continent will try to sell more here. Thirty years of high tariffs have given the British worker a protection of which he is not always conscious. So much so that Mr. William Rees-Mogg, City Editor of *The Sunday Times*, could write: "We still have a sentimental picture of British craftsmanship. In fact, the average British workman is technically under-educated by modern standards and the improvements in training and apprenticeship now being made are inadequate in quantity and not really satisfactory in quality."

The "national shake-up", recommended by Mr. Graham Hutton, must take place, not on the old party political lines but on a new economic and social basis. Class prejudice and class friction have kept the Trade Unions far more isolated from the higher ranks of management than their counterparts in the Six. Wage claims, labour disputes and strikes have always had a strong class flavour in Britain, fostered in the early days by the syndicalist element in the Labour movement and maintained since by the Socialist doctrinaires on the one hand and the extreme Left-Wing, or frankly Communist, elements on the other.

This has resulted in a completely haphazard approach to the vital question of wages and costs, an example of which is the leap-frogging of wage claims slammed in automatically after each Budget and in deliberate defiance, one is led to think, of appeals to restraint made by the Chancellor of the Exchequer of the day. The proud independence maintained by so many Unions *vis-à-vis* the TUC merely weakens the position of the latter when dealing with managements or with the Government. A strong case can be made out, under the Common Market, for the centralised planning of labour and a Government wages policy. But for this the Unions will have to put their own house in order first. They will have to impose much stronger discipline all the way down the line. If they do this, their leaders will have the authority necessary to represent them effectively in any planned labour and wages policy. If they do not, if they refuse to admit that there is a moral obligation on every worker in industry to pull his weight, then the future of labour relations will be bleak indeed. Nursing the suspicion that the Government has decided to join the Common

Market—even at the political price involved—solely because it had no other way of knocking the Unions' heads together will get nobody anywhere, least of all the working classes themselves who are the first victims of large-scale unemployment.

As for the individual Unions which are for or against joining the Common Market, it is too early at this stage to draw up a list. But it is fair to assume provisionally— until the full terms of membership are known—that the Transport and General Workers, the Chemical Workers, the Iron and Steel Confederation, the General and Municipal Workers and the Amalgamated Engineering Union are broadly in favour of joining, whilst the Agricultural workers, the Foundry workers and the Boilermakers have joined hands with the Shipbuilding and Engineering Confederation and the Association of Supervisory Staffs, Executives and Technicians, in opposing entry.

The Liberal Party

The Common Market problem has not ravaged the Liberal Party like it has the other two parties, (a) because its numbers are nothing like as great, and (b) because the European Community represents the sort of intellectual and practical internationalism that fits in so well with the Party's principles. Even before it had become obvious that the Six would have nothing to do with a marriage of any sort between the EEC and the EFTA, one of the Party's leading members, Mark Bonham Carter, son of Lady Violet, was advocating membership. Months before Britain sent in her application, the Liberals were urging the Government to stop sidling up to the problem and take the plunge. Liberals are not overworried at the loss of sovereignty because they believe that sovereignties must be merged in any case if Western civilisation is to survive the challenge from the East. There may be differences in the Party over the practical value of such all-encompassing institutions as the United Nations but there is no doubt in any Liberal's mind about the need for the Western European nations to pool their sovereignty in a Federal or Confederal United States of Europe. Had the Liberal Party's advice been taken earlier, the Government would have been in at the start and able to help fashion the institutions of the Community instead of fondly imagining, first, that it could wreck the whole project by getting tough and, second, that it could get the best of both worlds by linking up with the EEC on easy terms. As Sir Lionel Heald has rightly said: "Lookers-on may see most of the game, but they have no say in the result."

The Conservative Party

The Conservative Party provides the *pièce de résistance* in the Common Market drama because, traditionally, it has the largest "Primrose League" or "jingo" element in it. The peppery old Colonel, the austere ex-Naval Captain, the dashing young RAF officer, the gaitered cleric, the tweed-jacketed farmer, the pipe-smoking business executive, provide the social cadres of the Party. The wardrooms of HM ships, the clubrooms and messes of England, are no doubt today echoing with these noble words from Lord Selborne: "We might be more prosperous for a few years, but it would be at the expense of sacrificing what remains of our Imperial heritage, and with it our own future. The Continental nations may be charming neighbours and good friends, but they are not to be preferred to our own kith and kin who owe allegiance to the Queen and who thrice in my lifetime have sent their troops to fight alongside ours in desperate wars." Or with the following pithy words of wisdom from Mr. D. W. F. Nicholson, General Secretary of the British Association of Pig Producers: "We refuse to believe that the destiny of Great Britain is to submerge its identity—and its self-determination—in the stockpot of Europe. Neither Mr. Macmillan nor his Government has any sort of mandate from the British electorate to take such a step."

The "traditionalists" in the Party who oppose any close ties with the Continent are joined in some instances by men who lead or who are connected with trades or industries which might suffer from strong competition from abroad. Others feel that British industry on the whole is not yet geared to suffer such an outside challenge and must be given time to adjust itself before taking on the giants from Western Europe.

Yet others share the political doubts of some Labourites on the wisdom of becoming too closely associated with men like de Gaulle and Adenauer and assert that some of the West European nations are far too unstable for Britain to become associated with on a permanent basis.

The Prime Minister may have won a comfortable victory, on paper, in August, 1961, when the decision to apply for membership was first announced. Only one dyed-in-the-wool opponent of participation actually went into the lobbies against him. The others held their fire sheltering behind the very plausible excuse—which served the Labour Party in good stead—that not enough was known at the time about the conditions of entry. The battle within the Conservative Party will go on until these conditions are known. If the diehards suspect that the Government are getting the worst of the bargaining at Brussels with the Commission or with the Ministerial Council and that the conditions of admission are going to be tougher than was expected, then the anti-Common Marketeers may take courage *en bloc* and step up their campaign.

Only one Conservative—Mr. Anthony Fell, the Member for the Yarmouth Division of Norfolk—voted against the Government. The rest of the recalcitrants, 25 of them, abstained. One can only assume that the abstention was deliberate because they ignored a 3-line whip. They were: Sir John Barlow (Middleton and Prestwich), Sir Beverley Baxter (Southgate), Mr. Biggs-Davison (Chigwell), Mr. Richard Collard (Norfolk Central), Sir Eric Errington (Aldershot), Mr. Farey-Jones (Watford), Mr. J. A. Farr, (Harborough), Mr. George Forrest (Mid-Ulster), Sir Robert Grimston (Westbury), Viscount Hinchingbrooke (Dorset S.), Mr. J. H. Hollingworth (Birmingham, All Saints), Mr. Alan Hopkins (Bristol N.E), the Hon. Greville Howard (Cornwall, St. Ives), Mr. Robert Jenkins (Dulwich), Mr. J. C. Jennings (Burton), Captain Henry Kerby (Arundel & Shoreham), Mr. Anthony Marlowe (Hove), Cdr. Douglas Marshall, RNVR (Cornwall, Bodmin), Mr. Jasper More (Ludlow), Mr. Ian Percival (Southport), Mr. Ronald Russell (Wembley), the Rt. Hon. Robin Turton (Thirsk & Malton), Mr. Peter Walker (Worcester), Sir Derek Walker-Smith, QC (Herts. E.), Mr. Paul Williams (Sunderland, S.).

The Government were well aware of this deep cleavage of opinion within their own ranks yet still decided that on balance they should apply for membership. Why? At this short distance from events it is impossible to give the exact reasons. Only a few members of the Cabinet know with absolute certainty why it was decided to cross the Rubicon. But what evidence there is shows that the prospect of being politically isolated from Europe added to the decline in exports and the parlous state of the economy generally left the Government with no option. Lord Gladwyn's warning: "There is really no alternative to the Common Market" seems to have been driven home with great force in Whitehall.

.   .   .

What sort of a political Europe is Britain going into? Will it be a Federation or a Confederation of States? This question has not yet been resolved. It lurked in the background for years because it was too delicate to air in public particularly during the uncertain years which followed de Gaulle's advent to power in France. But at their meeting at Bad Godesberg in July, 1961, the Six decided that a Commission should study ways and means of giving "the unity of their peoples a statutory character" which means that some time in 1962 the full implications of Federalism or Confederalism will be known and a decision could be taken on how next to proceed. The "Federalists" are strong, particularly among members of the Commission and among supporters in all countries of a unitary Europe. The "Confederalists" are less ambitious and are concerned like the politicians with the need to carry Governments and a substantial majority of the people with them.

At all events, the approach is still functional in the sense that any political institutions will be grafted on to the Treaty of Rome. The old ideas of the supranational unitary state of the 1950s which received such a sharp blow when the French National Assembly threw out the European Defence Community are still in abeyance. The position is fluid and Britain's entry may yet, ironically enough, give General de Gaulle the support he needs for his ideas on Confederation in which a whittled down *Europe des patries* might find a convenient nestling-place. Even the Federalists who maintain that they are on the upswing realise that the Community can move no faster than the Governments of which it is composed. They are, however, the least enthusiastic about Britain's entry because they feel that the process of unification may be unduly slowed down. Britain, they say, is not boarding a stationary vehicle.

That there is a political commitment Britain must accept if and when she enters has been made clear by the, at present, "Confederalist", M. Couve de Murville, the French Foreign Minister, who said pointedly in the French Assembly on July 20, 1961: "I believe that today all our partners have arrived at the conclusion that the Common Market is not conceivable in the long run without some form of political union in Europe." And by the "Federalist" Professor Walter Hallstein, Chairman of the European Commission, who stated at Cambridge, Mass., USA, on May 22, 1961: "Joining the Community means a deep commitment to its Customs Union, to harmonisation of economic policy and to supporting its institutions with their supranational political character."

If Britain has at last resigned itself to accepting these political obligations, the one compelling reason, above all others, is undoubtedly to provide a counterweight to rising German influence and power in Europe. It was thought at one time, contrary, it might be said, to American thinking, that this counterweight could be provided from the outside without entailing membership of the Community. This theory has been proved false by the determination of the Six to go ahead with or without Britain. The hope of those who care for the future of Europe and its civilisation must be that the Six will go ahead *with* Britain and perhaps on to a greater Atlantic union such as that envisaged by Mr. Adlai Stevenson, M. Jean Monnet, and, one suspects, Mr. Macmillan.

Chapter Nine

WHAT THEY SAY

The following quotations have been taken from a variety of sources, but mostly from the Press. They represent a fair cross-section of the thinking public.

"There are far too many journalists talking about the 'eclipse' of this nation as a great Power. We have always, not least in Victorian times, had these 'little Englanders' who belittle the achievements of their country."—Sir Richard Pilkington, Conservative MP for Poole, Dorset.

"Our present economic position is untenable . . . in terms of industrial output, national product per head, exports, foreign currency reserves and productivity, we are the laggards of Western Europe."—Michael Gassman, Enfield, Middlesex.

"It is more important than ever that Britain should join the Common Market . . . most firms are anxiously waiting for the decision to be taken as the cost of setting up new factories on the Continent would be prohibitive to many."—James Priestman, Deputy Managing Director of Priestman Bros., excavator manufacturers, Hull.

"It is an odd argument that we should enter into the Common Market in order to compete, not against competitors who are weaker but against competitors who are stronger! Clearly we should make ourselves stronger before we enter, or we lose. But, if we do that, there is no need to enter at all."—Sir Lynn Ungoed-Thomas, QC, MP, Labour MP for Leicester, N.E.

"It is both futile and dishonest to pretend that this does not face Britain with the most fundamental decision in her history."—Denis Healey, Labour MP for Leeds, East.

"The Common Market is motivated by protectionist ideas . . . it is a very definite threat to all nations this side of the Iron Curtain which depend for their livelihood to any extent upon international trade."—Newton Jones, London.

"What we must not do is to join any organisation without a full understanding of its implications and then find ourselves being swept further than we intended. Once the decision is taken, it will be too late to complain."—The Earl of Avon (formerly Sir Anthony Eden).

"One of Britain's great contributions to civilisation has been in the development of political institutions. To link the Common Market and the Commonwealth is a task to which we can make a vital contribution."—Mark Bonham Carter, former Liberal MP for Torrington.

"Any expansion of trade resulting from Britain joining the Common Market would at the moment be at the expense of British manufacturers rather than to their advantage."—E. J. Steadman, Rickmansworth, Herts.

"The Government is not entitled to clamp this 'revolution' on the country without seeking a mandate for it at a general election."—Lord Elibank.

"The essential thing for us to do is to negotiate on the basis of a Common tariff and the political obligations of the Treaty of Rome."—Lord Gladwyn, former British Ambassador in Paris.

"Lord Gladwyn is putting an empty cart before a

bucking horse. Britain clearly cannot join the Common Market on Treaty of Rome terms or anything like them." —Mr. Maurice Petherick, Chairman, Commonwealth Industries Association.

"The economic potentialities of the Commonwealth are beyond comprehension. Already by far our largest market, the Commonwealth is also the least saturated of the world's markets."—Peter Walker, Andrew Bowden, Geoffrey Finsberg, Terence Wray, Nicholas Scott, all high-ranking Young Conservatives.

"The importance of the Commonwealth as regards intra-Commonwealth trade seems to be on the down-turn."—Mr. R. L. Willis, Joint Chairman of the Common Market Study Group of the Association of British Chambers of Commerce.

"I regard it as only the first step in something far bigger, comprising all free Europe, the Commonwealth and the Americas."—Paul Bryan, MP for Howden and Vice-Chairman of the Conservative Party Organisation.

"The world has become not too divided but too united; not only the two super powers but also powers of the more modest size of France, Germany or Great Britain are not too small but too big—far bigger than is necessary or even useful for the enjoyment of a good life."— Professor Leopold Kohr, University of Puerto Rico.

"In return for purely speculative economic gains, Britain would surrender control of her own agricultural, industrial and foreign policies to an unelected committee of foreigners on which her representative would sit in a minority of one, pledged to uphold a system geared to Continental requirements and operating according to Roman, not common law."—Mrs. Mary Howarth, Hamburg, Germany.

"The Rhineland Catholics have never aspired to a domination of the Common Market. They are as well by history as by their practical law much closer than anybody else in Germany to our western partners. On the contrary, they think that a full integration of Great Britain into the Common Market may cause to fade away any aspiration to dominate the Common Market some member or the other might nourish in her secret dreams."—Rudolf Werner, Member of the German Bundestag.

"There is no evidence that the Rome Treaty, except in the case of West Germany where improved economic conditions are due to other causes, has brought about a higher standard of living and economic stability, let alone anything approaching political stability."—Rt. Hon. Emanuel Shinwell, Labour MP for Easington.

"The greatest possible unity amongst the free countries of Europe linked with the Atlantic alliance is a political necessity of the highest priority."—Sir Edward Beddington-Behrens, Chairman, British Section, European League for Economic Co-operation, London.

"Are we going to forget the Commonwealth with more than 650 million people, with vast quantities of every raw material needed by man, with almost limitless possibilities of expansion?"—Hon. George Drew, Canadian High Commissioner in London.

"Do we want to get into the position of Canada where a continued trading deficit offset by capital investment has led to the majority of Canadian industry being owned by foreigners?"—Mr. John Paul, London.

"Most of the Commonwealth are determined to become industrialised in order to raise their standard of living. These infant industries will demand protection during the growing period, so increasing barriers against our goods and services must be expected—we have just seen that in Canada."—Sir Alex Spearman, Conservative MP for Scarborough and Whitby.

"The Commonwealth has a political and economic strength that could be realised and summoned to the beneficent use of mankind if there was a will to that end." —Mr. D. J. Killen, MP for Moreton, Brisbane, Australia.

"The Commonwealth has never been or claimed to be a political unit. Politically it is less of a unit than the average alliance, or even of the at present unallied states of Western Europe."—Sir William Hayter, former Deputy Under-Secretary of State at the Foreign Office and Warden of New College, Oxford.

"Has Sir William Hayter forgotten what we have owed to the Commonwealth in two world wars in his lifetime? Where were some leading members of the Six then? Actions sometimes count for more than votes."—Capt. John Litchfield, Conservative MP for Chelsea.

"If the Government arrive in the Common Market at all, it seems they will do so like a man standing backwards on an upward-moving escalator and occasionally taking a few steps down."—Mr. Roy Jenkins, Labour MP for Stechford, Warwickshire.

"Is the real proposition of the advocates of the Common Market that we cannot learn to be efficient without joining; in other words that we cannot earn our keep without being buttressed by more vigorous people?"— Mr. Richard Bethell, Managing Director, Bethell Brothers, Ltd., London.

"It would appear that most of the Commonwealth want to have their cake and eat it—free entry of their raw materials into the United Kingdom and yet maintain a high tariff on our manufactured goods into their own countries in order to protect their secondary industries." —Mr. D. E. Balme, London.

"If Britain joined the Common Market, the Americans would take over the Canadian, Australian and New Zealand markets; the Germans would take over the markets of India, the Middle East and perhaps Africa and we would be really a European off-shore island."— Mr. Clive Jenkins, General Secretary of the Association of Supervisory Staffs, Executives and Technicians.

"I cannot possibly believe that the Commonwealth countries such as Canada, Australia and New Zealand will suddenly decide to become one happy trading family."—Mr. W. D. Wieloch, Fulwood, Sheffield.

"In the Commonwealth it is still possible . . . to come to mutually advantageous arrangements by means of preferences negotiated with each country and adjusted to each as a producer and a consumer."—Commonwealth Industries Association.

"The stark fact is that, far from being open, the Commonwealth markets tend to make more difficult the entry of British manufactured goods, a tendency likely to gain impetus with the setting up of local Commonwealth industries."—Mr. B. F. Tobias, Nufloor, Ltd., Basildon, Essex.

"I am at a loss to understand how anyone who genuinely supports the ideals of the United Nations can fail to support the chance we now have of obtaining a dramatic advance towards a united Europe."—Mr. Arthur Holt, Liberal MP for Bolton, West.

"I am not sure I want Britain to join in a union of that kind (federal) with Western Germany under an Adenauer-like régime and France which is extremely unstable. God knows what will happen when de Gaulle dies. I think it is pretty risky from a political point of view us joining that kind of set-up."—Mr. Tom Driberg, Labour MP and Member of the Labour Party National Executive.

"The Common Market is likely to prove a better choice (than the Commonwealth or EFTA) for contemporary British farmers and farm workers and, in particular, for their sons."—A. N. Duckham, Professor of Agriculture, Reading University.

"The Common Market will be more of a bonanza for capitalism than anything seen in a lifetime."—Mr. Harold Davies, Labour MP for Leek.

"Entry by Britain into the European Economic Community will bring a breath of fresh air into the economic life of Britain and enable us to get rid of the restraints, restrictions, inhibitions and complacency which go with an economy which has become too introspective."—Mr. S. P. Chambers, Chairman, Imperial Chemical Industries.

VITAL STATISTICS

IN a world increasingly dominated by continental-sized economic and political groups, the European Community has emerged as a unit comparable in size both to the United States and the USSR. A recent issue of the "Bulletin Général de Statistiques", published by the Community's Statistical Office, from which the figures below have been taken, graphically illustrates this fact and compares some of the main features of the Community's economy with that of the United Kingdom. (Figures refer to 1959.)

	Community	UK	USA	USSR
Area (1,000 Km.²)	1,167	244	7,828	22,273
Population (millions)	168·5	52·0	177·7	212·3
Working Population (millions)	72·4	24·1	69·4	96·9
AGRICULTURE				
Cows (millions)	46·3	11·0	96·7	70·8
Total Cereal Production (million tons per year)	53·1	9·4	182·3	133·2
Cow Milk Production (million tons per year)	58·9	11·6	56·4	62·0
Number of Agricultural Tractors (000's)	1,805	434	4,750	996

	Community	UK	USA	USSR
ENERGY				
Coal Production (million tons per year)	234·9	209·4	388·4	365·4
Electricity Production (1,000m. KWH per year)	241·0	114·6	794·5	264·0
INDUSTRY				
Crude Steel Production (million tons per year)	63·2	20·5	84·8	59·9
Cement Production (million tons per year)	57·7	12·8	57·7	38·7
Passenger Car Production (1,000 per year)	3,106	1,190	5,599	125
Commercial Vehicles (1,000 per year)	400	370	1,124	371
SHIPPING				
Merchant Ships (million gross tons)	20·4	21·1	24·8	3·4
TRADE				
Imports CIF ($ billion)	24·3	11·2	15·2	5·1
Exports FOB ($ billion)	25·2	9·7	17·6	5·4

PRINCIPAL CLAUSES OF THE TREATY OF ROME

(*Note:* The Treaty also contains 4 Annexes, 9 Protocols and 1 Convention, all of which form an integral part of the Treaty.)

PREAMBLE TO THE TREATY

HIS MAJESTY THE KING OF THE BELGIANS, THE PRESIDENT OF THE FEDERAL REPUBLIC OF GERMANY, THE PRESIDENT OF THE FRENCH REPUBLIC, THE PRESIDENT OF THE ITALIAN REPUBLIC, HER ROYAL HIGHNESS THE GRAND DUCHESS OF LUXEMBOURG, HER MAJESTY THE QUEEN OF THE NETHERLANDS,

DETERMINED to establish the foundations of an ever closer union among the European peoples,

DECIDED to ensure the economic and social progress of their countries by common action in eliminating the barriers which divide Europe,

DIRECTING their efforts to the essential purpose of constantly improving the living and working conditions of their peoples,

RECOGNISING that the removal of existing obstacles calls for concerted action in order to guarantee a steady expansion, a balanced trade and fair competition,

ANXIOUS to strengthen the unity of their economies and to ensure their harmonious development by reducing the differences existing between the various regions and by mitigating the backwardness of the less favoured,

DESIROUS of contributing by means of a common commercial policy to the progressive abolition of restrictions on international trade,

INTENDING to confirm the solidarity which binds Europe and overseas countries, and desiring, to ensure the development of their prosperity, in accordance with the principles of the Charter of the United Nations,

RESOLVED to strengthen the safeguards of peace and liberty by establishing this combination of resources, and calling upon the other peoples of Europe who share their ideal to join in their efforts,

HAVE DECIDED to create a European Economic Community and to this end have designated as their plenipotentiaries;

HIS MAJESTY THE KING OF THE BELGIANS:

Mr. Paul-Henri SPAAK, Minister of Foreign Affaires,

Baron J. Ch. SNOY et d'OPPUERS, Secretary-General of the Ministry of Economic Affairs, Head of the Belgian delegation to the Inter-governmental Conference;

THE PRESIDENT OF THE FEDERAL REPUBLIC OF GERMANY:
Dr. Konrad ADENAUER, Federal Chancellor,
Professor Dr. Walter HALLSTEIN, State Secretary of the Federal Foreign Office;

THE PRESIDENT OF THE FRENCH REPUBLIC:
Mr. Christian PINEAU, Minister of Foreign Affairs,
Mr. Maurice FAURE, Under-Secretary of State for Foreign Affairs;

THE PRESIDENT OF THE ITALIAN REPUBLIC:
Mr. Antonio SEGNI, President of the Council of Ministers,
Professor Gaetano MARTINO, Minister of Foreign Affairs;

HER ROYAL HIGHNESS THE GRAND DUCHESS OF LUXEMBOURG:
Mr. Joseph BECH, Prime Minister, Minister of Foreign Affairs,
Mr. Lambert SCHAUS, Ambassador, Head of the Luxembourg delegation to the Intergovernmental Conference;

HER MAJESTY THE QUEEN OF THE NETHERLANDS:
Mr. Joseph LUNS, Minister of Foreign Affairs,
Mr. J. LINTHORST-HOMAN, Head of the Netherlands delegation to the Intergovernmental Conference;

WHO, having exchanged their full powers, found in good and due form, HAVE AGREED as follows:

ARTICLE 1

By the present Treaty, the HIGH CONTRACTING PARTIES establish among themselves a EUROPEAN ECONOMIC COMMUNITY.

ARTICLE 2

It shall be the aim of the Community, by establishing a Common Market and progressively approximating the economic policies of Member States, to promote throughout the Community a harmonious development of economic activities, a continuous and balanced expansion, an increased stability, an accelerated raising of the standard of living and closer relations between its Member States.

ARTICLE 3

For the purposes set out in the preceding Article, the activities of the Community shall include, under the conditions and with the timing provided for in this Treaty:

(a) the elimination, as between Member States, of customs duties and of quantitative restrictions in regard to the importation and exportation of goods, as well as of all other measures with equivalent effect;

(*b*) the establishment of a common customs tariff and *a common commercial policy towards third countries*;

(*c*) the abolition, as between Member States, of the obstacles to the free movement of persons, services and capital;

(*d*) the inauguration of a common agricultural policy;

(*e*) the inauguration of a common transport policy;

(*f*) the establishment of a system ensuring that competition shall not be distorted in the Common Market;

(*g*) the application of procedures which shall make it possible to co-ordinate the economic policies of Member States and to remedy disequilibria in their balances of payments;

(*h*) the approximation of their respective municipal law to the extent necessary for the functioning of the Common Market;

(*i*) the creation of a European Social Fund in order to improve the possibilities of employment for workers and to contribute to the raising of their standard of living;

(*j*) the establishment of a European Investment Bank intended to facilitate the economic expansion of the Community through the creation of new resources; and

(*k*) the association of overseas countries and territories with the Community with a view to increasing trade and to pursuing jointly their effort towards economic and social development.

ARTICLE 4

1. The achievement of the tasks entrusted to the Community shall be ensured by:

—an ASSEMBLY,
—a COUNCIL,
—a COMMISSION,
—a COURT OF JUSTICE.

Each of these institutions shall act within the limits of the powers conferred upon it by this Treaty.

2. The Council and the Commission shall be assisted by an *Economic and Social Committee* acting in a consultative capacity.

ARTICLE 5

Member States shall take all general or particular measures which are appropriate for ensuring the carrying out of the obligations arising out of this Treaty or resulting from the acts of the institutions of the Community. They shall facilitate the achievement of the Community's aims.

They shall abstain from any measures likely to jeopardise the attainment of the objectives of this Treaty.

ARTICLE 6

1. Member States, acting in close collaboration with the institutions of the Community, shall co-ordinate their respective economic policies to the extent that is necessary to attain the objectives of this Treaty.
2. The institutions of the Community shall take care not to prejudice the internal and external financial stability of Member States.

ARTICLE 7

Within the field of application of this Treaty and without prejudice to the special provisions mentioned therein, any discrimination on the grounds of nationality shall hereby be prohibited.

The Council may, acting by means of a qualified majority vote on a proposal of the Commission and after the Assembly has been consulted, lay down rules in regard to the prohibition of any such discrimination.

ARTICLE 8

1. The Common Market shall be progressively established in the course of a transitional period of twelve years.

The transitional period shall be divided into three stages of four years each; the length of each stage may be modified in accordance with the provisions set out below.
2. To each stage there shall be allotted a group of actions which shall be undertaken and pursued concurrently.
3. Transition from the first to the second stage shall be conditional upon a confirmatory statement to the effect that the essence of the objectives specifically laid down in this Treaty for the first stage has been in fact achieved and that, subject to the exceptions and procedures provided for in this Treaty, the obligations have been observed.

This statement shall be made at the end of the fourth year by the Council acting by means of a unanimous vote on a report of the Commission. The invocation by a Member State of the non-fulfilment of its own obligations shall not, however, be an obstacle to a unanimous vote. Failing a unanimous vote, the first stage shall automatically be extended for a period of one year.

At the end of the fifth year the Council shall make such confirmatory statement under the same conditions. Failing a unanimous vote, the first stage shall automatically be extended for a further period of one year.

At the end of the sixth year the Council shall make such a statement acting by means of a qualified majority vote on a report of the Commission.
4. Within a period of one month as from the date of this last vote, each Member State voting in a minority or, if the required majority

vote has not been obtained, any Member State, shall be entitled to require the Council to appoint an Arbitration Board whose decision shall bind all Member States and the institutions of the Community. The Arbitration Board shall be composed of three members appointed by the Council acting by means of a unanimous vote on a proposal of the Commission.

If the Council has not within a period of one month from the date of such requirement appointed the members of the Arbitration Board, they shall be appointed by the Court of Justice within a further period of one month.

The Arbitration Board shall appoint its Chairman.

The Board shall give its award within a period of six months from the date of the vote by the Council referred to in paragraph 3, last sub-paragraph.

5. The second and third stages may not be extended or curtailed except pursuant to a decision of the Council acting by means of a unanimous vote on a proposal of the Commission.

6. The provisions of the preceding paragraphs shall not have the effect of extending the transitional period beyond a total duration of fifteen years after the date of the entry into force of this Treaty.

7. Subject to the exceptions or deviations provided for in this Treaty, the expiry of the transitional period shall constitute the final date for the entry into force of all the rules laid down and for the completion of all the measures required for the establishment of the Common Market.

ARTICLE 9

1. The Community shall be based upon a Customs Union covering the exchange of all goods and comprising both the prohibition, as between Member States, of customs duties on importation and exportation and all charges with equivalent effect and the adoption of a common customs tariff in their relations with third countries.

2. The provisions of Chapter 1, Section 1 and Chapter 2 of this Title shall apply to products originating in Member States and also to products coming from third countries and having been entered for consumption in Member States.

THE CUSTOMS UNION

THE ELIMINATION OF CUSTOMS DUTIES AS BETWEEN MEMBER STATES

ARTICLE 12

Member States shall refrain from introducing, as between themselves, any new customs duties on importation or exportation or charges with equivalent effect and from increasing such duties or charges as they apply in their commercial relations with each other.

ARTICLE 13

1. Customs duties on importation in force between Member States shall be progressively abolished by them in the course of the transitional period under the conditions laid down in Articles 14 and 15.
2. Charges in force between Member States having an effect equivalent to customs duties on importation shall be progressively abolished by them in the course of the transitional period. The Commission shall, by means of directives, fix the timing of such abolition. It shall be guided by the rules mentioned in Article 14, paragraphs 2 and 3, and by the directives issued by the Council in application of the said paragraph 2.

ARTICLE 14

1. In respect of each product, the basic duty which shall be subject to the successive reductions shall be the duty applied on 1 January 1957.
2. The timing of the reductions shall be as follows:
  a) in the course of the first stage, the first reduction shall be made one year after the date of the entry into force of this Treaty; the second reduction shall be made eighteen months later; the third, at the end of the fourth year after the date of the entry into force of this Treaty;
  b) in the course of the second stage, a reduction shall be made eighteen months after the beginning of that stage; a second reduction eighteen months after the preceding one; a third reduction shall be made one year later; and
  c) the reductions which still remain to be made shall be carried out in the course of the third stage; the Council, acting by means of a qualified majority vote on a proposal of the Commission, shall fix their timing by means of directives.
3. At the time of the first reduction, Member States shall, in respect of each product, bring into force as between themselves a duty equal to the basic duty less 10 per cent.

At the time of each subsequent reduction, each Member State shall reduce the total of the duties in such a way as to reduce by 10 per cent its total customs receipts as defined in paragraph 4, it being understood that the reduction in the case of each product shall be equal to at least 5 per cent of the basic duty.

In respect of products, however, on which a duty of more than 30 per cent would still remain, each reduction shall be equal to not less than 10 per cent of the basic duty.

4. The total customs receipts of each Member State, referred to in paragraph 3, shall be calculated by multiplying by the basic duties the value of its imports coming from other Member States during the year 1956.

5. Any special problems raised by the application of the preceding paragraphs shall be settled by directives issued by the Council acting by means of a qualified majority vote on a proposal of the Commission.

6. Member States shall report to the Commission as to the manner in which the preceding rules for the reduction of duties are applied. They shall endeavour to ensure that the reduction applied to the duties on each product shall amount:

—at the end of the first stage to at least 25 per cent of the basic duty; and

—at the end of the second stage to at least 50 per cent of the basic duty.

If the Commission finds that there is a danger that the objectives laid down in Article 13 and the percentages fixed in this paragraph may not be achieved, it shall make any appropriate recommendations to the Member States.

7. The provisions of this article may be amended by the Council acting by means of a unanimous vote on a proposal of the Commission and after the Assembly has been consulted.

ARTICLE 15

1. Independently of the provisions of Article 14, any Member State may, in the course of the transitional period, suspend in whole or in part the collection of the duties applied by it to products imported from other Member States. It shall inform the other Member States and the Commission thereof.

2. Member States hereby declare their willingness to reduce their customs duties in regard to other Member States more rapidly than provided for in Article 14 if their general economic situation and the situation of the sector concerned so permit.

ESTABLISHMENT OF THE COMMON MARKET TARIFF

ARTICLE 18

Member States hereby declare their willingness to contribute to the development of international commerce and the reduction of barriers to trade by entering into reciprocal and mutually advantageous arrangements directed to the reduction of customs duties below the general level which they could claim as a result of the establishment of a Customs Union between themselves.

1. Under the conditions and within the limits laid down below, the duties under the common customs tariff shall be at the level of the arithmetical average of the duties applied in the four customs territories covered by the Community.

2. The duties taken into account for calculating this average shall be those applied by Member States on 1 January 1957.

In the case of the Italian tariff, however, the duty applied shall be understood as being that levied before the temporary 10 per cent reduction. Furthermore, in the case of tariff headings in regard to which this tariff contains a conventional duty, this duty shall be substituted for the duty applied as defined above, provided that it does not exceed the latter by more than 10 per cent. If the conventional duty exceeds the applied duty as defined above by more than 10 per cent, the latter duty, increased by 10 per cent, shall be taken into account for calculating the arithmetical average.

With regard to the tariff headings contained in List A, the duties shown in that List shall, for the purpose of calculating the arithmetical average, be substituted for the duties applied.

3. The duties under the common customs tariff shall not exceed:

a) 3 per cent in the case of products coming under the tariff headings mentioned in List B;

b) 10 per cent in the case of products coming under the tariff headings mentioned in List C;

c) 15 per cent in the case of products coming under the tariff headings mentioned in List D; and

d) 25 per cent in the case of products coming under the tariff headings mentioned in List E; where, in respect of such products, the tariff of the Benelux countries contains a duty of not more than 3 per cent, such duty shall, for the purpose of calculating the arithmetical average, be raised to 12 per cent.

4. The duties applicable to products mentioned in List F shall be those laid down therein.

5. The Lists of tariff headings referred to in this Article and in Article 20 shall be set out in Annex I to this Treaty.

ARTICLE 20

The duties applicable to the products in List G shall be fixed by means of negotiation between the Member States. Each Member State may add further products to this List up to the limit of 2 per cent of the total value of its imports coming from third countries in the course of the year 1956.

The Commission shall take all appropriate steps in order that such negotiations shall be undertaken before the end of the second year after the date of the entry into force of this Treaty and concluded before the end of the first stage ...

ARTICLE 23

For the purpose of the progressive introduction of the common customs tariff, Member States shall amend their tariffs applicable to third countries in the following manner:

a) in the case of tariff headings on which the duties in fact applied on 1 January 1957 do not differ by more than 15 per cent in either direction from the duties under the common customs tariff, the latter duties shall be applied at the end of the fourth year after the date of the entry into force of this Treaty;

b) in the case of the other tariff headings, each Member State shall, as from the same date, apply a duty which reduces by 30 per cent the difference between the duty in fact applied on 1 January 1957 and that under the common customs tariff;

c) at the end of the second stage this difference shall again be reduced by 30 per cent; and

d) in the case of tariff headings for which the duties under the common customs tariff are not yet known at the end of the first stage, each Member State shall, within a period of six months after the Council has acted in accordance with the provisions of Article 20, apply such duties as shall result from the application of the rules contained in this paragraph.

ARTICLE 26

The Commission may authorise any Member State encountering special difficulties to postpone the lowering or the raising, in accordance with the provisions of Article 23, of the duties on certain headings of its tariff.

Such authorisation may only be granted for a limited period and for tariff headings which together represent for such State not more than 5 per cent of the value of its total imports coming from third countries in the course of the latest year for which statistical data are available.

ARTICLE 29

In carrying out the tasks entrusted to it under this Section, the Commission shall be guided by:

a) the need for promoting commercial exchange between the Member States and third countries;

b) the development of competitive conditions within the Community to the extent to which such development will result in the increase of the competitive capacity of the enterprises;

c) the Community's requirements of supply in raw materials and semi-finished goods, while at the same time taking care not to distort competitive conditions between Member States with regard to finished goods; and

d) the need for avoiding serious disturbances in the economic life of Member States and for ensuring a rational development of production and an expansion of consumption within the Community.

THE ELIMINATION OF QUANTITATIVE RESTRICTIONS AS BETWEEN MEMBER STATES

ARTICLE 30

Quantitative restrictions on importation and all measures with equivalent effect shall, without prejudice to the following provisions, hereby be prohibited between Member States.

ARTICLE 31

Member States shall refrain from introducing as between themselves any quantitative restrictions or measures with equivalent effect.

This obligation shall, however, only apply to the level of liberalisation attained in application of the decisions of the Council of the Organisation for European Economic Co-operation of 14 January 1955. Member States shall communicate to the Commission, not later than six months after the date of the entry into force of this Treaty, the lists of the products liberalised by them in application of these decisions. The lists thus communicated shall be consolidated between Member States.

ARTICLE 32

Member States shall, in their mutual trade, refrain from making more restrictive the quotas or measures with equivalent effect in existence at the date of the entry into force of this Treaty.

ARTICLE 34

1. Quantitative restrictions on exportation and any measures with equivalent effect shall hereby be prohibited as between Member States.

2. Member States shall abolish, not later than at the end of the first stage, all quantitative restrictions on exportation and any measures with equivalent effect in existence at the date of the entry into force of this Treaty.

ARTICLE 37

Member States shall progressively adjust any State monopolies of a commercial character in such a manner as will ensure the exclusion, at the date of the expiry of the transitional period, of all discrimination between the nationals of Member States in regard to conditions of supply or marketing of goods.

AGRICULTURE

ARTICLE 38

1. The Common Market shall extend to agriculture and trade in agricultural products. Agricultural products shall mean the products of the soil, of stock-breeding and of fisheries as well as products after the first processing stage which are directly connected with such products.

2. Save where there are provisions to the contrary in Articles 39 to 46 inclusive, the rules laid down for the establishment of the Common Market shall apply to agricultural products.

3. Products subject to the provisions of Articles 39 to 46 inclusive are listed in Annex II to this Treaty. Within a period of two years after the date of the entry into force of this Treaty the Council, acting by means of a qualified majority vote on a proposal of the Commission shall decide as to the products to be added to that list.

4. The functioning and development of the Common Market in respect of agricultural products shall be accompanied by the establishment of a common agricultural policy among the Member States.

ARTICLE 39

1. The common agricultural policy shall have as its objectives:

a) to increase agricultural productivity by developing technical progress and by ensuring the rational development of agricultural production and the optimum utilisation of the factors of production, particularly labour;

b) to ensure thereby a fair standard of living for the agricultural population, particularly by the increasing of the individual earnings of persons engaged in agriculture;

c) to stabilise markets;

d) to guarantee regular supplies; and

e) to ensure reasonable prices in supplies to consumers.

2. In working out the common agricultural policy and the special methods which it may involve, due account shall be taken of:

a) the particular character of agricultural activities, arising from the social structure of agriculture and from structural and natural disparities between the various agricultural regions;

b) the need to make the appropriate adjustments gradually; and *c*) the fact that in Member States agriculture constitutes a sector which is closely linked with the economy as a whole.

ARTICLE 40

1. Member States shall gradually develop the common agricultural policy during the transitional period and shall establish it not later than at the end of that period.

2. With a view to achieving the objectives set out in Article 39, a common organisation of agricultural markets shall be effected.

This organisation shall take one of the following forms according to the products concerned:

a) common rules concerning competition;

b) compulsory co-ordination of the various national market organisations; or

c) a European market organisation.

3. The common organisation in one of the forms mentioned in paragraph 2 may comprise all measures necessary to achieve the objectives set out in Article 39, in particular, price controls, subsidies as to the production and marketing of various products, arrangements for stock-piling and carry-forward, and common machinery for stabilising importation or exportation.

The organisation shall confine itself to pursuing the objectives set out in Article 39 and shall exclude any discrimination between producers or consumers within the Community.

A common price policy, if any, shall be based on common criteria and on uniform methods of calculation.

4. In order to enable the common organisation referred to in paragraph 2 to achieve its objectives, one or more agricultural orientation and guarantee funds may be established.

ARTICLE 41

In order to permit the achievement of the objectives set out in Article 39, provision may be made within the framework of the common agricultural policy for, *inter alia*:

a) an effective co-ordination of efforts undertaken in the spheres of occupational training, research and the popularisation of rural economy, which may involve projects or institutions financed jointly; and

b) common action for the development of the consumption of certain products.

ARTICLE 42

The provisions of the Chapter relating to the rules of competition shall apply to the production of and trade in agricultural products only to the extent determined by the Council within the framework of the provisions and in accordance with the procedure laid down in Article 43, paragraphs 2 and 3, due account being taken of the objectives mentioned in Article 39.

The Council may, in particular, authorise the granting of aids:

a) for the protection of enterprises handicapped by structural or natural conditions; and

b) within the framework of economic development programmes.

ARTICLE 43

1. In order to formulate the guiding lines of a common agricultural policy, the Commission shall, upon the date of the entry into force of this Treaty, convene a conference of Member States, with a view to comparing their agricultural policies by drawing up, in particular, a statement of their resources and needs.

2. The Commission, taking due account of the work of the conference provided for in paragraph 1, shall, after consulting the Economic and Social Committee and within a period of two years after the date of the entry into force of this Treaty, submit proposals concerning the working out and putting into effect of the common agricultural policy, including the substitution of national organisations by one of the forms of common organisation provided for in Article 40, paragraph 2, as well as concerning the putting into effect of the measures specially mentioned under this Title.

These proposals shall take due account of the interdependence of the agricultural questions raised under this Title.

The Council, acting during the first two stages by means of a unanimous vote and subsequently by means of a qualified majority vote on a proposal of the Commission and after the Assembly has been consulted, shall issue regulations or directives or take decisions without prejudice to any recommendations which it may make.

3. The common organisation provided for in Article 40, paragraph 2, may, under the conditions provided for in the preceding paragraph, be substituted for national market organisations by the Council acting by means of a qualified majority vote:

a) if the common organisation offers to Member States which are opposed to this measure and which possess a national organisation of their own for the production concerned, equivalent guarantees regarding the employment and standard of living of the producers concerned, due account being taken of the time-factor in respect of possible adjustments and of necessary specialisations; and

b) if such organisation ensures for exchanges within the Community conditions similar to those existing in a domestic market.

4. If a common organisation is created for certain raw materials at a time when no common organisation yet exists for the corresponding processed products, the raw materials concerned which are used for processed products destined for export to third countries may be imported from outside the Community.

ARTICLE 44

1. In the course of the transitional period and to the extent that the progressive abolition of customs duties and quantitative restrictions between Member States may result in prices likely to jeopardise the achievement of the objectives set out in Article 39, each Member State shall be permitted to apply to certain products, in a non-discriminatory manner and in substitution for quotas, to such an extent as shall not impede the expansion of the volume of trade provided for in Article 45, paragraph 2, a system of minimum prices below which imports may be:

—temporarily suspended or reduced; or

—made conditional on their price being above the minimum price fixed for the product concerned.

In the second case, the minimum prices shall not include customs duties.

2. The minimum prices shall not be such as to lead to a reduction of exchanges existing between Member States at the date of the entry into force of this Treaty and shall not be an obstacle to a progressive expansion of such exchanges. The minimum prices shall not be applied in such a manner as to be an obstacle to the development of a natural preference between the Member States.

3. Upon the entry into force of this Treaty, the Council, acting on a proposal of the Commission, shall determine objective criteria for the establishment of minimum price systems and for the fixing of such prices.

The criteria shall, in particular, take account of average national costs of production in the Member State applying the minimum price, of the situation of the various enterprises in relation to such costs and of the need for promoting both the progressive improvement of agricultural operations and the adjustments and specialisations necessary within the Common Market.

The Commission shall also propose a procedure for revision of these criteria in order to take into account and accelerate technical progress and in order progressively to approximate prices within the Common Market.

These criteria and the procedure for revision shall be determined by means of a unanimous vote of the Council in the course of the first three years after the date of the entry into force of this Treaty.

4. Until the Council's decision takes effect, Member States may fix minimum prices on condition that they previously communicate them to the Commission and to the other Member States in order to enable them to submit their comments.

As soon as the Council has taken its decision, Member States shall fix minimum prices on the basis of the criteria established under the conditions mentioned above.

The Council, acting by means of a qualified majority vote on a proposal of the Commission may correct the decisions taken if they do not conform to the criteria so determined.

5. From the beginning of the third stage and in cases where it has not yet been possible in respect of certain products to establish the above objective criteria, the Council, acting by means of a qualified majority vote on a proposal of the Commission, may modify the minimum prices applied to these products.

6. At the expiry of the transitional period, a table of minimum prices still in force shall be drawn up. The Council, acting on a proposal of the Commission by means of a majority of nine votes in accordance with the weighting provided for in Article 148, paragraph 2, first sub-paragraph, shall determine the system to be applied within the framework of the common agricultural policy.

ARTICLE 45

Until the substitution of the national organisation by one of the forms of common organisation provided for in Article 40, paragraph 2, the development of exchanges in respect of products for which there exist in certain Member States:

—provisions designed to guarantee to national producers a sale of their production, and

—a need of imports,

shall be pursued by the conclusion of long-term agreements or contracts between exporting and importing Member States.

Such agreements or contracts shall be directed towards the progressive abolition of any discrimination in the application of these provisions to the various producers within the Community.

The conclusion of such agreements or contracts shall take place in the course of the first stage; due account shall be taken of the principle of reciprocity.

WORKERS

ARTICLE 48

1. The free movement of workers shall be ensured within the Community not later than at the date of the expiry of the transitional period.

2. This shall involve the abolition of any discrimination based on nationality between workers of the Member States as regards employment, remuneration, and other working conditions.

3. It shall include the right, subject to limitations justified by reasons of public order, public safety and public health:

a) to accept offers of employment actually made;

b) to move about freely for this purpose within the territory of Member States;

c) to stay in any Member State in order to carry on an employment in conformity with the legislative and administrative provisions governing the employment of the workers of that State; and

d) to live, on conditions which shall be the subject of implementing regulations to be laid down by the Commission, in the territory of a Member State after having been employed there.

4. The provisions of this Article shall not apply to employment in the public administration.

ARTICLE 50

Member States shall, under a common programme, encourage the exchange of young workers.

ARTICLE 51

The Council, acting by means of a unanimous vote on a proposal of the Commission, shall, in the field of social security, adopt the measures necessary to effect the free movement of workers, in particular, by introducing a system which permits an assurance to be given to migrant workers and their beneficiaries:

a) that, for the purposes of qualifying for and retaining the right to benefits and of the calculation of these benefits, all periods taken into consideration by the respective municipal law of the countries concerned, shall be added together; and

b) that these benefits will be paid to persons resident in the territories of Member States.

THE RIGHT OF ESTABLISHMENT

ARTICLE 52

Within the framework of the provisions set out below, restrictions on the freedom of establishment of nationals of a Member State in the territory of another Member State shall be progressively abolished in the course of the transitional period. Such progressive abolition shall also extend to restrictions on the setting up of agencies, branches or subsidiaries by nationals of any Member State established in the territory of any Member State.

Freedom of establishment shall include the right to engage in and carry on non-wage-earning activities, and also to set up and manage enterprises and, in particular, companies within the meaning of Article 58, second paragraph, under the conditions laid down by the law of the country of establishment for its own nationals, subject to the provisions of the Chapter relating to capital.

ARTICLE 53

Member States shall not, subject to the provisions of this Treaty, introduce any new restrictions on the establishment in their territories of nationals of other Member States.

ARTICLE 58

Companies constituted in accordance with the law of a Member State and having their registered office, central management or main establishment within the Community shall, for the purpose of applying the provisions of this Chapter, be assimilated to natural persons being nationals of Member States.

The term "companies" shall mean companies under civil or commercial law including co-operative companies and other legal persons under public or private law, with the exception of non-profit-making companies.

SERVICES

ARTICLE 59

Within the framework of the provisions set out below, restrictions on the free supply of services within the Community shall be progressively abolished in the course of the transitional period in respect of nationals of Member States who are established in a State of the Community other than that of the person to whom the services are supplied.

The Council, acting by means of a unanimous vote on a proposal of the Commission, may extend the benefit of the provisions of this Chapter to cover services supplied by nationals of any third country who are established within the Community.

ARTICLE 60

Services within the meaning of this Treaty shall be deemed to be services normally supplied for remuneration, to the extent that they are not governed by the provisions relating to the free movement of goods, capital and persons.

Services shall include in particular:

a) activities of an industrial character;

b) activities of a commercial character;

c) artisan activities; and

d) activities of the liberal professions.

Without prejudice to the provisions of the Chapter relating to the right of establishment, a person supplying a service may, in order to carry out that service, temporarily exercise his activity in the State where the service is supplied, under the same conditions as are imposed by that State on its own nationals.

ARTICLE 61

1. The free movement of services in respect of transport shall be governed by the provisions of the Title relating to transport.

2. The liberalisation of banking and insurance services connected with movements of capital shall be effected in harmony with the progressive liberalis ation of the movement of capital.

CAPITAL

ARTICLE 67

1. Member States shall, in the course of the transitional period and to the extent necessary for the proper functioning of the Common Market, progressively abolish as between themselves restrictions on the movement of capital belonging to persons resident in Member States and also any discriminatory treatment based on the nationality or place of residence of the parties or on the place in which such capital is invested.

2. Current payments connected with movements of capital between Member States shall be freed from all restrictions not later than at the end of the first stage.

ARTICLE 68

1. Member States shall, in respect of the matters referred to in this Chapter, grant in the most liberal manner possible such exchange authorisations as are still necessary after the date of the entry into force of this Treaty.

2. Where a Member State applies its domestic provisions in respect of the capital market and credit system to the movements of capital freed in accordance with the provisions of this Chapter, it shall do so in a non-discriminatory manner.

3. Loans intended for the direct or indirect financing of a Member State or of its territorial sub-divisions may not be issued or placed in other Member States save when the States concerned have reached agreement in this respect. This provision shall not be an obstacle to the implementation of Article 22 of the Protocol on the Statute of the European Investment Bank.

ARTICLE 74

The objectives of this Treaty shall, with regard to the subject covered by this Title, be pursued by the Member States within the framework of a common transport policy.

ARTICLE 75

1. With a view to implementing Article 74 and taking due account of the special aspects of transport, the Council, acting on a proposal of the Commission and after the Economic and Social Committee and the Assembly have been consulted, shall, until the end of the second stage by means of a unanimous vote and subsequently by means of a qualified majority vote, lay down:

a) common rules applicable to international transport effected from or to the territory of a Member State or crossing the territory of one or more Member States;

b) conditions for the admission of non-resident carriers to national transport services within a Member State; and

c) any other appropriate provisions.

2. The provisions referred to under *(a)* and *(b)* of the preceding paragraph shall be laid down in the course of the transitional period.

3. Notwithstanding the procedure provided for in paragraph 1, provisions which relate to the principles governing transport and the application of which might seriously affect the standard of living and the level of employment in certain regions and also the utilisation of transport equipment, shall, due account being taken of the need for adaptation to economic developments resulting from the establishment of the Common Market, be laid down by the Council acting by means of a unanimous vote.

ARTICLE 84

1. The provisions of this Title shall apply to transport by rail, road and inland waterway.

2. The Council, acting by means of a unanimous vote, may decide whether, to what extent and by what procedure appropriate provisions might be adopted for sea and air transport.

ARTICLE 85

1. The following shall be deemed to be incompatible with the Common Market and shall hereby be prohibited: any agreement between enterprises, any decisions by associations of enterprises and any concerted practices which are likely to affect trade between the Member States and which have as their object or result the prevention, restriction or distortion of competition within the Common Market, in particular those consisting in:

a) the direct or indirect fixing of purchase or selling prices or of any other trading conditions;

b) the limitation or control of production, markets, technical development or investment;

c) market-sharing or the sharing of sources of supply;

d) the application to parties to transactions of unequal terms in respect of equivalent supplies, thereby placing them at a competitive disadvantage; or

e) the subjecting of the conclusion of a contract to the acceptance by a party of additional supplies which, either by their nature or according to commercial usage, have no connection with the subject of such contract.

2. Any agreements or decisions prohibited pursuant to this Article shall be null and void.

3. Nevertheless, the provisions of paragraph 1 may be declared inapplicable in the case of:

—any agreements or classes of agreements between enterprises,

—any decisions or classes of decisions by associations of enterprises, and

—any concerted practices or classes of concerted practices which contribute to the improvement of the production or distribution of goods or to the promotion of technical or economic progress while reserving to users an equitable share in the profit resulting therefrom, and which:

a) neither impose on the enterprises concerned any restrictions not indispensable to the attainment of the above objectives;

b) nor enable such enterprises to eliminate competition in respect of a substantial proportion of the goods concerned.

ARTICLE 86

To the extent to which trade between any Member States may be affected thereby, action by one or more enterprises to take improper advantage of a dominant position within the Common Market or within a substantial part of it shall be deemed to be incompatible with the Common Market and shall hereby be prohibited.

Such improper practices may, in particular, consist in:

a) the direct or indirect imposition of any inequitable purchase or selling prices or of any other inequitable conditions;

b) the limitation of production, markets or technical development to the prejudice of consumers;

c) the application to parties to transactions of unequal terms in respect of equivalent supplies, thereby placing them at a competitive disadvantage; or

d) the subjecting of the conclusion of a contract to the acceptance, by a party, of additional supplies which, either by their nature or according to commercial usage, have no connection with the subject of such contract.

DUMPING PRACTICES

ARTICLE 91

1. If, in the course of the transitional period, the Commission, at the request of a Member State or of any other interested party, finds that dumping practices exist within the Common Market, it shall issue recommendations to the originator or originators of such practices with a view to bringing them to an end.

Where such dumping practices continue, the Commission shall authorise the Member State injured to take protective measures of which the Commission shall determine the conditions and particulars.

2. Upon the entry into force of this Treaty, any products originating or having been entered for consumption in one Member State which have been exported to another Member State shall be admitted free of all customs duties, quantitative restrictions or measures with equivalent effect when re-imported into the territory of the first State. The Commission shall lay down appropriate rules for the application of this paragraph.

AIDS GRANTED BY STATES

ARTICLE 92

1. Except where otherwise provided for in this Treaty, any aid, granted by a Member State or granted by means of State resources, in any manner whatsoever, which distorts or threatens to distort competition by favouring certain enterprises or certain productions shall, to the extent to which it adversely affects trade between Member States, be deemed to be incompatible with the Common Market.

2. The following shall be deemed to be compatible with the Common Market:

a) aids of a social character granted to individual consumers, provided that such aids are granted without any discrimination based on the origin of the products concerned;

b) aids intended to remedy damage caused by natural calamities or other extraordinary events; or

c) aids granted to the economy of certain regions of the Federal Republic of Germany affected by the division of Germany, to the extent that such aids are necessary in order to compensate for the economic disadvantages caused by such division.

3. The following may be deemed to be compatible with the Common Market:

a) aids intended to promote the economic development of regions where the standard of living is abnormally low or where there exists serious under-employment;

b) aids intended to promote the execution of important projects of common European interest or to remedy a serious disturbance of the economy of a Member State;

c) aids intended to facilitate the development of certain activities or of certain economic regions, provided that such aids do not change trading conditions to such a degree as would be contrary to the common interest. Any aids to shipbuilding existing on 1 January 1957 shall, to the extent that such aids merely offset the absence of customs protection, be progressively reduced under the same conditions as apply to the abolition of customs duties, subject to the provisions of this Treaty relating to the common commercial policy in regard to third countries; and

d) such other categories of aids as may be specified by decision of the Council acting by means of a qualified majority vote on a proposal of the Commission.

FISCAL PROVISIONS

ARTICLE 95

A Member State shall not impose, directly or indirectly, on the products of other Member States any internal charges of any kind in excess of those applied directly or indirectly to like domestic products.

Furthermore, a Member State shall not impose on the products of other Member States any internal charges of such a nature as to afford indirect protection to other productions.

Member States shall, not later than at the beginning of the second stage, abolish or amend any provisions existing at the date of the entry into force of this Treaty which are contrary to the above rules.

The Commission shall consider in what way the law of the various Member States concerning *turnover taxes, excise duties and other forms of indirect taxation,* including compensatory measures applying to exchanges between Member States, can be harmonised in the interest of the Common Market.

The Commission shall submit proposals to the Council which shall act by means of a unanimous vote, without prejudice to the provisions of Articles 100 and 101.

APPROXIMATION OF LAWS

ARTICLE 100

The Council, acting by means of a unanimous vote on a proposal of the Commission, shall issue directives for the approximation of such legislative and administrative provisions of the Member States as have a direct incidence on the establishment or functioning of the Common Market.

The Assembly and the Economic and Social Committee shall be consulted concerning any directives whose implementation in one or more of the Member States would involve amendment of legislative provisions.

ARTICLE 101

Where the Commission finds that a disparity existing between the legislative or administrative provisions of the Member States distorts the conditions of competition in the Common Market and thereby causes a state of affairs which must be eliminated, it shall enter into consultation with the interested Member States.

If such consultation does not result in an agreement which eliminates the particular distortion, the Council, *acting during the first stage* by means of a unanimous vote and subsequently by means of a qualified majority vote on a proposal of the Commission, shall issue the directives necessary for this purpose. The Commission and the Council may take any other appropriate measures as provided for in this Treaty.

POLICY RELATING TO ECONOMIC TRENDS

ARTICLE 103

1. Member States shall consider their policy relating to economic trends as a matter of common interest. They shall consult with each other and with the Commission on measures to be taken in response to current circumstances.

2. Without prejudice to any other precedures provided for in this Treaty, the Council may, by means of a unanimous vote on a proposal of the Commission, decide on measures appropriate to the situation.

3. The Council, acting by means of a qualified majority vote on a proposal of the Commission, shall, where necessary, issue any requisite directives concerning the particulars of application of the measures decided upon under the terms of paragraph 2.

4. The procedures provided for in this Article shall apply also in the event of difficulties arising in connection with the supply of certain products.

BALANCE OF PAYMENTS

ARTICLE 104

Each Member State shall pursue the economic policy necessary to ensure the equilibrium of its overall balance of payments and to maintain confidence in its currency, while ensuring a high level of employment and the stability of the level of prices.

ARTICLE 105

1. In order to facilitate the attainment of the objectives stated in Article 104, Member States shall co-ordinate their economic policies. They shall for this purpose institute a collaboration between the competent services of their administrative departments and between their central banks.

The Commission shall submit to the Council recommendations for the bringing into effect of such collaboration.

2. In order to promote the co-ordination of the policies of Member States in monetary matters to the full extent necessary for the functioning of the Common Market, a *Monetary Committee* with consultative status shall hereby be established with the following tasks:

—to keep under review the monetary and financial situation of Member states and of the Community and also the general payments system of Member States and to report regularly thereon to the Council and to the Commission; and

—to formulate opinions, at the request of the Council or of the Commission or on its own initiative, for submission to the said institutions.

The Member States and the Commission shall each appoint two members of the Monetary Committee.

1. Each Member State shall treat its policy with regard to *exchange rates* as a matter of common interest.

2. If a Member State alters its exchange rate in a manner which is incompatible with the objectives laid down in Article 104 and which seriously distorts the conditions of competition, the Commission may, after consulting the Monetary Committee, authorise other Member States to take for a strictly limited period the necessary measures, of which it shall determine the conditions and particulars, in order to deal with the consequences of such alteration.

ARTICLE 108

1. Where a Member State is in difficulties or seriously threatened with difficulties as regards its balance of payments as a result either of overall disequilibrium of the balance of payments or of the kinds of currency at its disposal and where such difficulties are likely, in particular, to prejudice the functioning of the Common Market or the progressive establishment of the common commercial policy, the Commission shall without delay examine the situation of such State and the action which, in making use of all the means at its disposal, that State has taken or may take in conformity with the provisions of Article 104. The Commission shall indicate the measures which it recommends to the State concerned to adopt.

If the action taken by a Member State and the measures suggested by the Commission do not prove sufficient to overcome the difficulties encountered or threatening, the Commission shall, after consulting the Monetary Committee, recommend to the Council the granting of mutual assistance and the appropriate methods therefor.

The Commission shall keep the Council regularly informed of the situation and of its development.

2. The Council, acting by means of a qualified majority vote, shall grant mutual assistance; it shall issue directives or decisions laying down the conditions and particulars thereof. Mutual assistance may take the form, in particular, of:

a) concerted action in regard to any other international organisations to which Member States may have recourse;

b) any measures necessary to avoid diversions of commercial traffic where the State in difficulties maintains or re-establishes quantitative restrictions with regard to third countries; or

c) the granting of limited credits by other Member States, subject to the agreement of the latter.

Furthermore, during the transitional period, mutual assistance may also take the form of special reductions in customs duties or enlargements of quotas, for the purpose of facilitating the increase of imports from the State in difficulties, subject to the agreement of the States by which such measures would have to be taken.

3. If the mutual assistance recommended by the Commission is not granted by the Council or if the mutual assistance granted and the measures taken are insufficient, the Commission shall authorise the State in difficulties to take measures of safeguard of which the Commission shall determine the conditions and particulars.

Such authorisation may be revoked and such conditions and particulars may be amended by the Council acting by means of a qualified majority vote.

ARTICLE 109

1. Where a sudden crisis in the balance of payments occurs and if a decision, within the meaning of Article 108, paragraph 2, is not immediately taken, the Member State concerned may provisionally take the necessary measures of safeguard. Such measures shall cause the least possible disturbance in the functioning of the Common Market and shall not exceed the minimum strictly necessary to remedy the sudden difficulties which have arisen.

2. The Commission and the other Member States shall be informed of such measures of safeguard not later than at the time of their entry into force. The Commission may recommend to the Council mutual assistance under the terms of Article 108.

3. On the basis of an opinion of the Commission and after consulting the Monetary Committee, the Council, acting by means of a qualified majority vote, may decide that the State concerned shall amend, suspend or abolish the measures of safeguard referred to above.

COMMERCIAL POLICY

ARTICLE 110

By establishing a Customs Union between themselves the Member States intend to contribute, in conformity with the common interest, to the harmonious development of world trade, the progressive abolition of restrictions on international exchanges and the lowering of customs barriers.

The common commercial policy shall take into account the favourable incidence which the abolition of customs duties as between Member States may have on the increase of the competitive strength of the enterprises in those States.

ARTICLE 111

In the course of the transitional period and without prejudice to Articles 115 and 116, the following provisions shall apply:

1. Member States shall co-ordinate their commercial relations with third countries in such a way as to bring about, not later than at the expiry of the transitional period, the conditions necessary to the implementation of a common policy in the matter of external trade.

The Commission shall submit to the Council proposals regarding the procedure to be applied, in the course of the transitional period, for the establishment of common action and regarding the achievement of a uniform commercial policy.

2. The Commission shall submit to the Council recommendations with a view to tariff negotiations with third countries concerning the common customs tariff.

The Council shall authorise the Commission to open such negotiations.

The Commission shall conduct these negotiations in consultation with a special Committee appointed by the Council to assist the Commission in this task and within the framework of such directives as the Council may issue to it.

3. The Council shall, when exercising the powers conferred upon it under this Article, act during the first two stages by means of a unanimous vote and *subsequently by means of a qualified majority vote.*

4. Member States shall, in consultation with the Commission, take all necessary measures with the object, in particular, of adjusting their tariff agreements in force with third countries in order that the entry into force of the common customs tariff may not be delayed.

5. Member States shall aim at securing uniformity between themselves at as high a level as possible of their lists of liberalisation in regard to third countries or groups of third countries. For this purpose the Commission shall make any appropriate recommendations to Member States.

If Member States abolish or reduce quantitative restrictions in regard to third countries, they shall inform the Commission beforehand and shall accord identical treatment to the other Member States.

ARTICLE 112

1. Without prejudice to obligations undertaken by Member States within the framework of other international organisations, their measures to aid exports to third countries shall be progressively harmonised before the end of the transitional period to the extent necessary to ensure that competition between enterprises within the Community shall not be distorted.

On a proposal of the Commission, the Council, acting until the end of the second stage by means of a unanimous vote and subsequently by means of a qualified majority vote, shall issue the directives necessary for this purpose.

2. The preceding provisions shall not apply to such drawbacks on customs duties or charges with equivalent effect nor to such refunds of indirect charges including turnover taxes, excise duties and other indirect taxes as are accorded in connection with exports of goods from a Member State to a third country, to the extent that such drawbacks or refunds do not exceed the charges which have been imposed, directly or indirectly, on the products exported.

ARTICLE 113

1. After the expiry of the transitional period, the common commercial policy shall be based on uniform principles, particularly in regard to tariff amendments, the conclusion of tariff or trade agreements, the alignment of measures of liberalisation, export policy and protective commercial measures including measures to be taken in cases of dumping or subsidies.

2. The Commission shall submit proposals to the Council for the putting into effect of this common commercial policy.

3. Where agreements with third countries require to be negotiated, the Commission shall make recommendations to the Council, which will authorise the Commission to open the necessary negotiations.

The Commission shall conduct these negotiations in consultation with a special Committee appointed by the Council to assist the Commission in this task and within the framework of such directives as the Council may issue to it.

4. The Council shall, when exercising the powers conferred upon it by this Article, act by means of a qualified majority vote.

ARTICLE 114

The agreements referred to in Article 111, paragraph 2, and in Article 113 shall be concluded on behalf of the Community by the Council acting during the first two stages by means of a unanimous vote and subsequently by means of a qualified majority vote.

ARTICLE 115

In order to ensure that the execution of measures of commercial policy taken in conformity with this Treaty by any Member State shall not be prevented by diversions of commercial traffic, or where disparities between such measures lead to economic difficulties in one or more of the Member States, the Commission shall recommend the methods whereby the other Member States shall provide the necessary co-operation. Failing this, the Commission shall authorise the Member States to take the necessary protective measures of which it shall determine the conditions and particulars.

In cases of emergency and during the transitional period, Member States may themselves take such necessary measures and shall notify them to the other Member States and also to the Commission which may decide that the State concerned shall amend or revoke such measures.

In choosing such measures, priority shall be given to those which cause the least disturbance to the functioning of the Common Market and which take due account of the necessity for expediting, as far as possible, the introduction of the common customs tariff.

ARTICLE 116

As from the end of the transitional period, Member States shall in respect of all matters of particular interest in regard to the Common Market, within the framework of any international organisations of an economic character, only proceed by may of common action. The Commission shall for this purpose submit to the Council, which shall act by means of a qualified majority vote, proposals concerning the scope and implementation of such common action.

During the transitional period, Member States shall consult with each other with a view to concerting their action and, as far as possible, adopting a uniform attitude.

SOCIAL PROVISIONS

ARTICLE 117

Member States hereby agree upon the necessity to promote improvement of the living and working conditions of labour so as to permit the equalisation of such conditions in an upward direction.

They consider that such a development will result not only from the functioning of the Common Market which will favour the harmonisation of social systems, but also from the procedures provided for under this Treaty and from the approximation of legislative and administrative provisions.

ARTICLE 118

Without prejudice to the other provisions of this Treaty and in conformity with its general objectives, it shall be the aim of the Commission to promote close collaboration between Member States in the social field, particularly in matters relating to:

—employment,

—labour legislation and working conditions,

--occupational and continuation training,

—social security,

—protection against occupational accidents and diseases,

—industrial hygiene,

—the law as to trade unions, and collective bargaining between employers and workers.

For this purpose, the Commission shall act in close contact with Member States by means of studies, the issuing of opinions, and the organising of consultations both on problems arising at the national level and on those of concern to international organisations.

Before issuing the opinions provided for under this Article, the Commission shall consult the Economic and Social Committee.

ARTICLE 119

Each Member State shall in the course of the first stage ensure and subsequently maintain the application of the principle of equal remuneration for equal work as between men and women workers.

For the purposes of this Article, remuneration shall mean the ordinary basic or minimum wage or salary and any additional emoluments whatsoever payable directly or indirectly, whether in cash or in kind, by the employer to the worker and arising out of the workers' employment.

Equal remuneration without discrimination based on sex means:

a) that remuneration for the same work at piece-rates shall be calculated on the basis of the same unit of measurement; and

b) that remuneration for work at time-rates shall be the same for the same job.

ARTICLE 120

Member States shall endeavour to maintain the existing equivalence of paid holiday schemes.

THE EUROPEAN SOCIAL FUND

ARTICLE 123

In order to improve opportunities of employment of workers in the Common Market and thus contribute to raising the standard of living, a European Social Fund shall hereby be established in accordance with the provisions set out below; it shall have the task of promoting within the Community employment facilities and the geographical and occupational mobility of workers.

ARTICLE 124

The administration of the Fund shall be incumbent on the Commission.

The Commission shall be assisted in this task by a Committee presided over by a Member of the Commission and composed of representatives of Governments, trade unions and employers' associations.

ARTICLE 125

At the request of a Member State, the Fund shall, within the framework of the rules provided for in Article 127, cover 50 per cent of expenses incurred after the entry into force of this Treaty by that State or by a body under public law for the purpose of:

ARTICLE 129

A European Investment Bank having legal personality shall hereby be established.

The Members of the European Investment Bank shall be the Member States.

The Statute of the European Investment Bank shall form the subject of a Protocol annexed to this Treaty.

ARTICLE 130

The task of the European Investment Bank shall be to contribute, by calling on the capital markets and its own resources, to the balanced and smooth development of the Common Market in the interest of the Community. For this purpose, the Bank shall by granting loans and guarantees on a non-profit-making basis facilitate the financing of the following projects in all sectors of the economy:

a) projects for developing less developed regions,

b) projects for modernising or converting enterprises or for creating new activities which are called for by the progressive establishment of the Common Market where such projects by their size or nature cannot be entirely financed by the various means available in each of the Member States; and

c) projects of common interest to several Member States which by their size or nature cannot be entirely financed by the various means available in each of the Member States.

OVERSEAS TERRITORIES

ARTICLE 131

The Member States hereby agree to bring into association with the Community the non-European countries and territories which have special relations with Belgium, France, Italy and the Netherlands. These countries and territories, hereinafter referred to as "the countries and territories", are listed in Annex IV to this Treaty.

The purpose of this association shall be to promote the economic and social development of the countries and territories and to establish close economic relations between them and the Community as a whole.

In conformity with the principles stated in the Preamble to this Treaty, this association shall in the first place permit the furthering of the interests and prosperity of the inhabitants of these countries and territories in such a manner as to lead them to the economic, social and cultural development which they expect.

INSTITUTIONS

THE ASSEMBLY

ARTICLE 137

The Assembly, which shall be composed of representatives of the peoples of the States united within the Community, shall exercise the powers of deliberation and of control which are conferred upon it by this Treaty.

ARTICLE 138

1. The Assembly shall be composed of delegates whom the Parliaments shall be called upon to appoint from among their Members in accordance with the procedure laid down by each Member State.

2. The number of these delegates shall be fixed as follows:

Belgium	14
Germany	36
France	36
Italy	36
Luxembourg	6
Netherlands	14

3. The Assembly shall draw up proposals for election by direct universal suffrage in accordance with a uniform procedure in all Member States.

The Council, acting by means of a unanimous vote, shall determine the provisions which it shall recommend to Member States for adoption in accordance with their respective constitutional rules.

ARTICLE 139

The Assembly shall hold an annual session. It shall meet as of right on the third Tuesday in October.

The Assembly may meet in extraordinary session at the request of a majority of its members or at the request of the Council or of the Commission.

ARTICLE 140

The Assembly shall appoint its President and its officers from among its members.

Members of the Commission may attend all meetings and shall, at their request, be heard on behalf of the Commission.

The Commission shall reply orally or in writing to questions put to it by the Assembly or its members.

The Council shall be heard by the Assembly under the conditions which the Council shall lay down in its rules of procedure.

ARTICLE 141

Except where otherwise provided for in this Treaty, the Assembly shall act by means of an absolute majority of the votes cast.

The quorum shall be laid down in the rules of procedure.

ARTICLE 144

If a motion of censure concerning the activities of the Commission is introduced in the Assembly, a vote may be taken thereon only after a period of not less than three days following its introduction, and such vote shall be by open ballot.

If the motion of censure is adopted by a two-thirds majority of the votes cast, representing a majority of the members of the Assembly, the members of the Commission shall resign their office in a body. They shall continue to carry out current business until their replacement in accordance with the provisions of Article 158 has taken place.

THE COUNCIL

ARTICLE 145

With a view to ensuring the achievement of the objectives laid down in this Treaty, and under the conditions provided for therein, the Council shall:

—ensure the co-ordination of the general economic policies of the Member States; and

—dispose of a power of decision.

ARTICLE 146

The Council shall be composed of representatives of the Member States. Each Government shall delegate to it one of its members.

The office of President shall be exercised for a term of six months by each member of the Council in rotation according to the alphabetical order of the Member States.

ARTICLE 147

Meetings of the Council shall be called by the President acting on his own initiative or at the request of a member or of the Commission.

ARTICLE 148

1. Except where otherwise provided for in this Treaty, the conclusions of the Council shall be reached by a majority vote of its members.

2. Where conclusions of the Council require a qualified majority, the votes of its members shall be weighted as follows:

Belgium	2
Germany	4
France	4
Italy	4
Luxembourg	1
Netherlands	2

Majorities shall be required for the adoption of any conclusions as follows:

—twelve votes in cases where this Treaty requires a previous proposal of the Commission, or

—twelve votes including a favourable vote by at least four members in all other cases.

3. Abstentions by members either present or represented shall not prevent the adoption of Council conclusions requiring unanimity.

ARTICLE 149

When, pursuant to this Treaty, the Council acts on a proposal of the Commission, it shall, where the amendment of such proposal is involved, act only by means of a unanimous vote.

As long as the Council has not so acted, the Commission may amend its original proposal, particularly in cases where the Assembly has been consulted on the proposal concerned.

THE COMMISSION

ARTICLE 155

With a view to ensuring the functioning and development of the Common Market, the Commission shall:

—ensure the application of the provisions of this Treaty and of the provisions enacted by the institutions of the Community in pursuance thereof;

—formulate *recommendations* or *opinions* in matters which are the subject of this Treaty, where the latter expressly so provides or where the Commission considers it necessary;

—under the conditions laid down in this Treaty dispose of a power of *decision* of its own and participate in the preparation of acts of the Council and of the Assembly; and

—exercise the competence conferred on it by the Council for the implementation of the rules laid down by the latter.

ARTICLE 156

The Commission shall annually, not later than one month before the opening of the Assembly session, publish a general report on the activities of the Community.

ARTICLE 157

1. The Commission shall be composed of nine members chosen for their general competence and of indisputable independence.

The number of members of the Commission may be amended by a unanimous vote of the Council.

Only nationals of Member States may be members of the Commission.

The Commission may not include more than two members having the nationality of the same State.

2. The members of the Commission shall perform their duties in the general interest of the Community with complete independence.

In the performance of their duties, they shall not seek or accept instructions from any Government or other body. They shall refrain from any action incompatible with the character of their duties. Each Member State undertakes to respect this character and not to seek to influence the members of the Commission in the performance of their duties.

The members of the Commission may not, during their term of office, engage in any other paid or unpaid professional activity. When entering upon their duties, they shall give a solemn undertaking that, both during and after their term of office, they will respect the obligations resulting therefrom and in particular the duty of exercising honesty and discretion as regards the acceptance, after their term of office, of certain functions or advantages. Should these obligations not be respected, the Court of Justice, on the application of the Council or of the Commission, may according to circumstances rule that the member concerned either be removed from office in accordance with the provisions of Article 160 or forfeit his right to a pension or other advantages in lieu thereof.

ARTICLE 158

The members of the Commission shall be appointed by the Governments of Member States acting in Common agreement.

Their term of office shall be for a period of four years. It shall be renewable.

ARTICLE 161

The President and the two Vice-Presidents of the Commission shall be appointed from among its members for a term of two years in accordance with the same procedure as that laid down for the appointment of members of the Commission. Their term of office shall be renewable.

Except in the case of an entire renewal of the Commission, such appointments shall be made after the Commission has been consulted.

In the event of resignation or death, the President and the Vice-Presidents shall be replaced for the remainder of their terms of office in accordance with the procedure laid down in the first paragraph of this Article.

ARTICLE 162

The Council and the Commission shall consult each other and shall settle by mutual agreement the particulars of their collaboration.

The Commission shall adopt its rules of procedure with a view to ensuring its own functioning and that of its services in accordance with the provisions of this Treaty. It shall be responsible for the publication of its rules of procedure.

ARTICLE 163

The conclusions of the Commission shall be reached by a majority of the number of members provided for in Article 157.

A meeting of the Commission shall only be valid if the number of members laid down in its rules of procedure are present.

THE COURT OF JUSTICE

ARTICLE 164

The Court of Justice shall ensure observance of law and justice in the interpretation and application of this Treaty.

ARTICLE 165

The Court of Justice shall be composed of seven judges.

The Court of Justice shall sit in plenary session. It may, however, set up chambers, each composed of three or five judges, in order either to conduct certain enquiries or to judge certain categories of cases in accordance with provisions to be laid down in rules for this purpose.

The Court of Justice shall, however, always sit in plenary session in order to hear cases submitted to it by a Member State or by one of the institutions of the Community or to deal with preliminary questions submitted to it pursuant to Article 177.

Should the Court of Justice so request, the Council may, by means of a unanimous vote, increase the number of judges and make the requisite amendments to the second and third paragraphs of this Article and to Article 167, second paragraph.

ARTICLE 169

If the Commission considers that a Member State has failed to fulfil any of its obligations under this Treaty, it shall give a reasoned opinion on the matter after requiring such State to submit its comments.

If such State does not comply with the terms of such opinion within the period laid down by the Commission, the latter may refer the matter to the Court of Justice.

ARTICLE 170

Any Member State which considers that another Member State has failed to fulfil any of its obligations under this Treaty may refer the matter to the Court of Justice.

Before a Member State institutes, against another Member State, proceedings relating to an alleged infringement of the obligations under this Treaty, it shall refer the matter to the Commission.

The Commission shall give a reasoned opinion after the States concerned have been required to submit their comments in written and oral pleadings.

If the Commission, within a period of three months after the date of reference of the matter to it, has not given an opinion, reference to the Court of Justice shall not thereby be prevented.

ARTICLE 171

If the Court of Justice finds that a Member State has failed to fulfil any of its obligations under this Treaty, such State shall take the measures required for the implementation of the judgment of the Court.

ARTICLE 173

The Court of Justice shall review the lawfulness of acts other than recommendations or opinions of the Council and the Commission. For this purpose, it shall be competent to give judgment on appeals by a Member State, the Council or the Commission on grounds of incompetence, of errors of substantial form, of infringement of this Treaty or of any legal provision relating to its application, or of abuse of power.

Any natural or legal person may, under the same conditions, appeal against a decision addressed to him or against a decision which, although in the form of a regulation or a decision addressed to another person, is of direct and specific concern to him.

The appeals provided for in this Article shall be lodged within a period of two months dating, as the case may be, either from the publication of the act concerned or from its notification to the appellant or, failing that, from the day on which the latter had knowledge of that act.

ARTICLE 175

In the event of the Council or the Commission in violation of this Treaty failing to act, the Member States and the other institutions of the Community may refer the matter to the Court of Justice with a view to establishing such violation.

Such appeal shall only be admissible if the institution concerned has previously been invited to act. If, at the expiry of a period of two months after such invitation, that institution has not stated its attitude, the appeal may be lodged within a further period of two months.

Any natural or legal person may submit to the Court of Justice, under the conditions laid down in the preceding paragraphs, a complaint to the effect that one of the institutions of the Community has failed to address to him an act other than a recommendation or an opinion.

ARTICLE 177

The Court of Justice shall be competent to make a preliminary decision concerning:

a) the interpretation of this Treaty;

b) the validity and interpretation of acts of the institutions of the Community; and

c) the interpretation of the statutes of any bodies set up by an act of the Council, where such statutes so provide.

Where any such question is raised before a court or tribunal of one of the Member States, such court or tribunal may, if it considers that its judgment depends on a preliminary decision on this question, request the Court of Justice to give a ruling thereon.

Where any such question is raised in a case pending before a domestic court or tribunal from whose decisions no appeal lies under municipal law, such court or tribunal shall refer the matter to the Court of Justice.

ARTICLE 180

The Court of Justice shall be competent, within the limits laid down below, to hear cases concerning:

a) The fulfilment by Member States of the obligations arising under the Statute of the European Investment Bank. The Board of Directors of the Bank shall, in this respect, dispose of the powers conferred upon the Commission by Article 169;

b) the conclusions of the Board of Governors of the Bank. Any Member State, the Commission or the Board of Directors of the Bank may lodge an appeal in this matter under the conditions laid down in Article 173; and

c) the conclusions of the Board of Directors of the Bank. Appeals against such conclusions may be lodged, under the conditions laid down in Article 173, provided that they may only be lodged by a Member State or by the Commission, and only on the grounds of an infringement of formal procedures laid down in Article 21, paragraph 2 and paragraphs 5 to 7 inclusive of the Statute of the Bank.

ARTICLE 182

The Court of Justice shall be competent to decide in any dispute between Member States in connection with the object of this Treaty, where such dispute is submitted to it under the terms of a compromise.

ARTICLE 187

The judgments of the Court of Justice shall be enforceable under the conditions laid down in Article 192.

PROVISIONS COMMON TO SEVERAL INSTITUTIONS

ARTICLE 189

For the achievement of their aims and under the conditions provided for in this Treaty, the Council and the Commission shall adopt regulations and directives, make decisions and formulate recommendations or opinions.

Regulations shall have a general application. They shall be binding in every respect and directly applicable in each Member State.

Directives shall bind any Member State to which they are addressed, as to the result to be achieved, while leaving to domestic agencies a competence as to form and means.

Decisions shall be binding in every respect for the addressees named therein.

Recommendations and *opinions* shall have no binding force.

ARTICLE 191

The regulations shall be published in the *Official Journal of the Community*. They shall enter into force on the date fixed in them or, failing this, on the twentieth day following their publication.

Directives and decisions shall be notified to their addressees and shall take effect upon such notification.

Decisions of the Council or of the Commission which contain a pecuniary obligation on persons other than States shall be enforceable.

Forced execution shall be governed by the rules of civil procedure in force in the State in whose territory it takes place. The writ of execution shall be served, without other formality then the verification of the authenticity of the written act, by the domestic authority which the Government of each Member State shall designate for this purpose and of which it shall give notice to the Commission and to the Court of Justice.

After completion of these formalities at the request of the party concerned, the latter may, in accordance with municipal law, proceed with such forced execution by applying directly to the authority which is competent.

Forced execution may only be suspended pursuant to a decision of the Court of Justice. Supervision as to the regularity of the measures of execution shall, however, be within the competence of the domestic courts or tribunals.

THE ECONOMIC AND SOCIAL COMMITTEE

ARTICLE 193

There shall hereby be established an Economic and Social Committee with consultative status.

The Committee shall be composed of representatives of the various categories of economic and social life, in particular, representatives of producers, agriculturists, transport operators, workers, merchants, artisans, the liberal professions and of the general interest.

ARTICLE 194

The number of members of the Committee shall be fixed as follows:

Belgium	12
Germany	24
France	24
Italy	24
Luxembourg	5
Netherlands	12

The members of the Committee shall be appointed for a term of four years by the Council acting by means of a unanimous vote. This term shall be renewable.

The members of the Committee shall be appointed in their personal capacity and shall not be bound by any mandatory instructions.

ARTICLE 197

The Committee shall include specialised sections for the main fields covered by this Treaty.

It shall contain, in particular, an agricultural section and a transport section, which are the subject of special provisions included in the Titles relating to agriculture and transport.

These specialised sections shall operate within the framework of the general competence of the Committee. They may not be consulted independently of the Committee.

ARTICLE 210

The Community shall have legal personality.

ARTICLE 211

The Community shall in each of the Member States possess the most extensive legal capacity accorded to legal persons under their respective municipal law; it may, in particular, acquire or transfer movable and immovable property and may sue and be sued in its own name. For this purpose, the Community shall be represented by the Commission.

ARTICLE 213

For the performance of the tasks entrusted to it, the Commission may collect any information and verify any matters within the limits and under the conditions laid down by the Council in accordance with the provisions of this Treaty.

ARTICLE 217

The rules concerning the languages of the institutions of the Community shall, without prejudice to the provisions laid down in the rules of the Court of Justice, be determined by the Council acting by means of a unanimous vote.

ARTICLE 218

The Community shall, under conditions defined in a separate Protocol, enjoy in the territories of the Member States the privileges and immunities necessary for the achievement of its aims.

ARTICLE 219

Member States undertake not to submit a dispute concerning the interpretation or application of this Treaty to any method of settlement other than those provided for in this Treaty.

ARTICLE 220

Member States shall, in so far as necessary, engage in negotiations with each other with a view to ensuring for the benefit of their nationals:

—the protection of persons as well as the enjoyment and protection of rights under the conditions granted by each State to its own nationals;

—the elimination of double taxation within the Community;

—the mutual recognition of companies within the meaning of Article 58, second paragraph, the maintenance of their legal personality in cases where the registered office is transferred from one country to another, and the possibility for companies subject to the municipal law of different Member States to form mergers; and

—the simplification of the formalities governing the reciprocal recognition and execution of judicial decisions and of arbitral awards.

ARTICLE 223

1. The provisions of this Treaty shall not detract from the following rules:

a) No Member State shall be obliged to supply information the disclosure of which it considers contrary to the essential interests of its security.

b) Any Member State may take the measures which it considers necessary for the protection of the essential interests of its security, and which are connected with the production of or trade in arms, ammunition and war material; such measures shall not, however, prejudice conditions of competition in the Common Market in respect of products not intended for specifically military purposes.

2. In the course of the first year after the date of the entry into force of this Treaty, the Council, acting by means of a unanimous vote, shall determine the list of products to which the provisions of paragraph 1 (*b*) shall apply.

3. The Council, acting by means of a unanimous vote on a proposal of the Commission, may amend the said list.

ARTICLE 224

Member States shall consult one another for the purpose of enacting in common the necessary provisions to prevent the functioning of the Common Market from being affected by measures which a Member State may be called upon to take in case of serious internal disturbances affecting public order, in case of war or serious international tension constituting a threat of war or in order to carry out undertakings into which it has entered for the purpose of maintaining peace and international security.

ARTICLE 226

1. In the course of the transitional period, where there are serious difficulties which are likely to persist in any sector of economic activity of difficulties which may seriously impair the economic situation in any region, a Member State may ask for authorisation to take measures of safeguard in order to restore the situation and adapt the sector concerned to the Common Market economy.

2. At the request of the State concerned, the Commission shall by an expedited procedure immediately determine the measures of safeguard which it considers necessary, specifying the conditions and particulars of application.

3. The measures authorised under paragraph 2 may include derogations from the provisions of this Treaty, to the extent and for the periods strictly necessary for the achievement of the objects referred to in paragraph 1. Priority shall be given in the choice of such measures to those which will least disturb the functioning of the Common Market.

ARTICLE 228

1. Where this Treaty provides for the conclusion of agreements between the Community and one or more States or an international organisation, such agreements shall be negotiated by the Commission. Subject to the powers conferred upon the Commission in this field, such agreements shall be concluded by the Council after the Assembly has been consulted in the cases provided for by this Treaty.

The Council, the Commission or a Member State may, as a preliminary, obtain the opinion of the Court of Justice as to the compatibility of the contemplated agreements with the provisions of this Treaty. An agreement which is the subject of a negative opinion of the Court of Justice may only enter into force under the conditions laid down, according to the case concerned, in Article 236.

2. Agreements concluded under the conditions laid down above shall be binding on the institutions of the Community and on Member States.

ARTICLE 229

The Commission shall be responsible for ensuring all suitable contacts with the organs of the United Nations, of their Specialised Agencies and of the General Agreement on Tariffs and Trade.

The Commission shall also ensure appropriate contacts with all international organisations.

ARTICLE 230

The Community shall establish all suitable co-operation with the Council of Europe.

ARTICLE 231

The Community shall establish with the Organisation for European Economic Co-operation close collaboration, the particulars of which shall be determined by common agreement.

ARTICLE 234

The rights and obligations resulting from conventions concluded prior to the entry into force of this Treaty between one or more Member States, on the one hand, and one or more third countries, on the other hand, shall not be effected by the provisions of this Treaty.

In so far as such conventions are not compatible with this Treaty, the Member State or States concerned shall take all appropriate steps to eliminate any incompatibility found to exist. Member States shall, if necessary, assist each other in order to achieve this purpose and shall, where appropriate, adopt a common attitude.

Member States shall, in the application of the conventions referred to in the first paragraph, take due account of the fact that the advantages granted under this Treaty by each Member State form an integral part of the establishment of the Community and are therefore inseparably linked with the creation of common institutions, the conferring of competences upon such institutions and the granting of the same advantages by all other Member States.

ARTICLE 235

If any action by the Community appears necessary to achieve, in the functioning of the Common Market, one of the aims of the community in cases where this Treaty has not provided for the requisite powers of action, the Council, acting by means of a unanimous vote on a proposal of the Commission and after the Assembly has been consulted, shall enact the appropriate provisions.

ARTICLE 236

The Government of any Member State or the Commission may submit to the Council proposals for the revision of this Treaty.

If the Council, after consulting the Assembly and, where appropriate, the Commission, expresses an opinion in favour of the calling of a conference of representatives of the Governments of Member States, such conference shall be convened by the President of the Council for the purpose of determining in common agreement the amendments to be made to this Treaty.

Such amendments shall enter into force after being ratified by all Member States in accordance with their respective constitutional rules.

ARTICLE 237

Any European State may apply to become a member of the Community. It shall address its application to the Council which, after obtaining the opinion of the Commission, shall act by means of a unanimous vote.

The conditions of admission and the adjustments to this Treaty necessitated thereby shall be the subject of an agreement between the Member States and the applicant State. Such agreement shall be submitted to all the contracting States for ratification in accordance with their respective constitutional rules.

ARTICLE 238

The Community may conclude with a third country, a union of States or an international organisation agreements creating an association embodying reciprocal rights and obligations, joint actions and special procedures.

Such agreements shall be concluded by the Council acting by means of a unanimous vote and after consulting the Assembly.

Where such agreements involve amendments to this Treaty, such amendments shall be subject to prior adoption in accordance with the procedure laid down in Article 236.

ARTICLE 240

This Treaty shall be concluded for an unlimited period.

ARTICLE 248

The present Treaty, drawn up in a single original in the German, French, Italian and Netherlands languages, all four texts being equally authentic, shall be deposited in the archives of the Government of the Italian Republic which shall transmit a certified copy to each of the Governments of the other signatory States.

IN FAITH WHEREOF, the undersigned Plenipotentiaries have placed their signatures at the end of the present Treaty.

Done at Rome, on the twenty-fifth day of March in the year one thousand nine hundred and fifty-seven.

P. H. SPAAK.	J. Ch. SNOY et d'OPPUERS.
ADENAUER.	HALLSTEIN.
PINEAU.	M. FAURE.
Antonio SEGNI.	Gaetano MARTINO.
BECH.	Lambert SCHAUS.
J. LUNS.	J. LINTHORST-HOMAN.